Trojan Women

THE TROJAN WOMEN BY EURIPIDES
AND HELEN AND ORESTES BY RITSOS

Translated by Gwendolyn MacEwen
and Nikos Tsingos

Exile Editions, Toronto

This edition is published by Exile Editions Limited, 69 Sullivan Street, Toronto, Ontario M5T 1C2

Sales and distribution: General Publishing Co. Ltd., 30 Lesmill Road, Don Mills, Ontario M3B 2T6.

Drawing by John Gould.

ISBN 0-920428-26-6

Trojan Women

Contents

Helen

A POEM BY YANNIS RITSOS

Translated by Gwendolyn MacEwen
and Nikos Tsingos

(Even from a distance the wear and tear showed — crumbling walls with fallen plaster; faded window-shutters; the balcony railings rusted. A curtain stirring outside the window on the upper floor, yellowed, frayed at the bottom. When he approached — hesitantly — he found the same sense of desolation in the garden: disorderly plants, voluptuous leaves, unpruned trees; the odd flower choked in the nettles; the waterless fountains, mouldy; lichen on the beautiful statues. An immobile lizard between the breasts of a young Aphrodite, basking in the last rays of the setting sun. How many years had passed! He was so young then — twenty-two? twenty-three? And she? You could never tell — she radiated so much light, it blinded you; it pierced you through — you couldn't tell anymore what she was, if she was, if you were. He rang the doorbell. Standing in the place he once knew so well, now so strangely changed with its unknown entanglement of dark colors, he heard the sound of the bell ringing, solitary. They were slow to answer the door. Someone peered out from the upper window. It wasn't her. A servant, very young. Apparently laughing. She left the window. Still no answer at the door. Afterwards footsteps were heard inside on the stairway. Someone unlocked the door. He went up. A smell of dust, rotten fruit, dried-up slop, urine. Over here. Bedroom. Wardrobe. Metal mirror. Two tottering carved arm-chairs. A small cheap tin table with coffee cups and cigarette butts. And she? No, no, impossible! An old, old woman — one, two hundred years old! But five years ago — Oh no! The bedsheet full of holes. There, unstirring; sitting on the bed; bent over. Only her eyes — larger than ever, autocratic, penetrating, vacant.)

Yes, yes – it's me. Sit down for a while. Nobody comes around
    anymore. I'm starting
to forget how to use words. Anyway, words don't matter. I think
    summer's coming,
the curtains are stirring differently – they're – trying to say something –
    such stupidities! One of them
has already flown out of the window, straining to break the rings,
to fly over the trees – maybe as well to haul
the whole house away – but the house resists with all corners
and me along with it, despite the fact that I've felt for months,
    liberated
from my dead ones, my own self, and this resistance of mine,
incomprehensible, beyond my will, strange to me, is all I possess –
    my wedlock
with this bed, this curtain – is also my fear, as though
my whole body were sustained by the ring with the black stone I
    wear on my forefinger

Now, I examine this stone very closely now in these endless hours
    of night –
it's black, it has no reflections – it grows, it grows, it fills up
with black waters – the waters overflow, swell; I sink,
not to the bottom, but to an upper depth; from up there
I can make out my room down below, myself, the wardrobe, the servants
quibbling voicelessly; I see one of them perched
on a stool and with a hard, spiteful expression,
polishing the photograph of Leda; I see the duster leaving behind
a trail of dust and delicate bubbles which rise and burst
with quiet murmuring all around my ankle-bones or knees.

I notice you also have a perplexed, dumbfounded face, distorted
by the slow undulations of black water – now widening, now
    lengthening your face
with yellow streaks. Your hair's writhing upwards
like an upside down Medusa. But then I say: it's only a stone,
a small precious stone. All the blackness contracts, then
dries up and localizes in the smallest possible knot – I feel it
here, just under my throat. And I'm back again
in my room, on my bed, beside my familiar phials

9

which stare at me, one by one, nodding – only they can help me
for insomnia, fear, memories, forgetfulness, asthma.

What are you up to? Still in the army? Be careful. Don't
     distress yourself so much
about heroism, honors and glories. What'll you do with them?
     Do you still have
that shield on which you had my face engraved? You were so funny
in your tall helmet with its long tail – so very young,
and shy, as though you'd concealed your handsome face
between the hind legs of a horse whose tail hung all the way down
your bare back. Don't get mad again. Stay awhile longer.

The time of antagonism is over now; desires have dried up;
perhaps now, together, we can observe the same point of futility –
where, I think, the only true encounters are realized – however
     indifferent,
but nonetheless soothing – our new community, bleak, quiet, empty,
without much displacement or opposition – let's just stir the ashes
     of the fireplace,
making now and again long thin lovely burial urns
or sit down on the ground and beat it with soundless palms.

Little by little things lost their meaning, became empty; did
they ever perhaps mean anything? – slack, hollow;
we stuffed them with straw and chaff, to give them form,
let them thicken, solidify, stand firmly – the tables, chairs,
the bed we lay on, the words; always hollow
like the cloth sacks, the vendors' burlap bags;
from the outside you can already make out what's inside them,
potatoes, onions, wheat, corn, almonds, or flour.

Sometimes one of them catches on a nail on the stair
or on the prong of an anchor down in the harbor, it rips open,
the flour spills out – a foolish river. The bag empties itself.
The poor gather up the flour in handfuls to make
some pies or gruel. The bag collapses. Someone

picks it up from its two bottom ends; shakes it out in the air;
a cloud of white dust enfolds him; his hair turns white;
especially his eyebrows turn white. The others watch him.
They don't understand a thing; they wait for him to open his mouth,
    to say something.
He doesn't. He folds up the bag into four sections; he leaves
as he is, white, inexplicable, wordless, as though disguised
as a lewd naked man covered with a sheet,
or like a cunning dead man resurrected in his shroud.

So, events and things don't have any meaning — the same goes for
    words, although
with words we name, more or less, those things we lack, or which
we've never seen — airy, as we say, eternal things —
innocent words, misleading, consoling, equivocal, always
trying to be correct — what a terrible thing,
to have named a shadow, invoking it at night in bed
with the sheet pulled up to your neck, and hearing it, we fools
    think
that we're holding our bodies together, that they're holding us,
    that we're keeping our hold on the world.

Nowadays I forget the names I knew best or get them all mixed up —
Paris, Menelaus, Achilles, Proteus, Theoklymenos, Tefkros,
Castor and Polydeuces — my moralizing brothers; who, I gather
have turned into stars — so they say — pilot-lights for ships —
    Theseus, Pireitheus,
Andromache, Cassandra, Agamemnon — sounds, only formless sounds,
their images unwritten on a window-pane
or a metal mirror or on the shallows of a beach, like that time
on a quiet sunny day, with myriads of masts, after the battle
had abated, and the creaking of the wet ropes on the pulleys
hauled the world up high, like the knot of a sob arrested
in a crystalline throat — you could see it sparkling, trembling
without becoming a scream, and suddenly the entire landscape, the
    ships,
the sailors and the chariots, were sinking into light and anonymity.

Now, another deeper, darker submersion – out of which
some sounds emerge now and then – when hammers were pounding wood
and nailing together a new trireme in a small shipyard; when a huge
four-horse chariot was passing by on the stone road, adding to
    the ticks
from the cathedral clock in another duration, as though
there were more, much more than twelve hours and the horses
were turning around in the clock until they were exhausted; or when
    one night
two handsome young men were singing below my windows
a song for me, without words – one of them one-eyed; the other
wearing a huge buckle on his belt – gleaming in the moonlight.

Words don't come to me on their own now – I search them out as
    though I'm translating
from a language I don't know – nevertheless, I do translate.
    Between the words,
and within them, are deep holes; I peer through them as though
I'm peering through the knots which have fallen from the boards
    of a door
completely closed up, nailed here for ages. I don't see a thing.

No more words or names; I can only single out some sounds – a
    silver candlestick
or a crystal vase rings by itself and all of a sudden stops,
pretending it knows nothing, that it didn't ring, that nobody
struck it, or passed by it. A dress
collapses softly from the chair onto the floor, diverting
attention from the previous sound to the simplicity of nothing.
    However
the idea of a silent conspiracy, although diffused in air,
floats densely higher up, almost *immeasurable,*
so that you feel the etching of the lines around your mouth grow
    deeper
precisely because of this presence of an intruder who takes over
    your position
turning you into an intruder, right here on your own bed, in your
    own room.

Oh, to be alienated in our very clothes which get old,
in our own skin which gets wrinkled; while our fingers
can no longer grip or even wrap around our bodies
the blanket which rises by itself, disperses, disappears, leaving
    us
bare before the void. Then, the guitar hanging on the wall
with its rusty strings, forgotten for years, begins to quiver
like the jaw of an old woman quivering from cold or fear, and
you have to put your palm flat upon the strings to stop
the contagious chill. But you can't find your hand, you don't
    have one;
and you hear in your guts that it's your own jaw that's shaking.

In this house the air's become heavy and inexplicable, maybe
due to the natural presence of the dead. A trunk opens
on its own, old dresses fall out, rustle, stand up straight
and quietly stroll around; two gold tassels remain on the carpet;
    a curtain
opens — revealing nobody — but they're still there; a cigarette
burns on and off in the ashtray; the person who
left it there is in the other room, rather awkward,
his back turned, gazing at the wall, possibly at a spider
or a damp stain, facing the wall, so the dark
hollow under his protruding cheekbones won't show.

The dead feel no pain for us any more — that's odd, isn't it? —
not so much for them as for us — that neutral intimacy of theirs
within a place which has rejected them and where they don't
    contribute
a thing to the upkeep, nor concern themselves with the run-down
    condition,
them, accomplished and unchangeable, and yet seeming somewhat larger.

This is what sometimes confounds us — the augmentation of the
    unchangeable
and their silent self-sufficiency — not at all haughty; they don't
    try
to force you to remember them, to be pleasing. The women

let their bellies slacken; their stockings sagging, they take
the pins from the silver box; they stick them in the sofa's velvet
one by one, in two straight rows; then pick them up
and begin again with the same polite attention. Someone who's
     very tall
emerges from the hall – he knocks his head against the door;
he doesn't make a single grimace – and neither could the knock be
     heard at all.

Yes, they're as foolish as we; only quieter. Another of them
raises his arm ceremoniously, as though to give a blessing to
     someone,
pulls off a piece of the crystal from the chandelier, puts it in his
     mouth
simply, like glass fruit – you think he's going to chew it, to get
     a human function
in motion again – but no; he clenches it between his teeth, thus,
to let the crystal shine with a futile brightness. A woman
takes some face-cream from the little round white jar
with a skilled movement of two of her fingers, and writes
two thick capital letters on the windowpane – they look like L and D –
the sun heats the glass pane, the cream melts, drips down the wall –
and all this means nothing – just two greasy, brief furrows.

I don't know why the dead stay around here without anyone's sympathy;
     I don't know what they want
wandering around the rooms in their best clothes, their best shoes
polished, immaculate, yet noiselessly as though they never touch
     the floor.
They take up space, sprawl wherever they like, in the two rocking
     chairs,
down on the floor, or in the bathroom; they forget and leave the tap
     dripping;
forget the perfumed bars of soap melting in the water. The servants
passing among them, sweeping with the big broom,
don't notice them. Only sometimes, the laughter of a maid
somewhat confined – it doesn't fly up, out of the window,
it's like a bird tied by the leg with a string, which someone is
     pulling downward.

Then the servants get inexplicably furious with me, they throw the broom
    here, right into the middle of my room, and go into the kitchen;
    I hear them
making coffee in big briquets, spilling the sugar on the floor —
it crunches under their shoes; the aroma of the coffee
drifts through the hallway, floods the house, observes itself
in the mirror like a silly, dark, impudent face covered with uncombed
    tufts of hair
and two false skyblue earrings, blows its breath on the mirror,
clouds the glass. I feel my tongue probing around in my mouth;
I feel that I've still got some saliva. 'A coffee for me too,' —
    I call to the servants;
'a coffee,' (that's all I ask for; I don't want anything else).
    They
act as though they don't hear. I call over and over again
without bitterness or rage. They don't answer. I hear them
gulping down their coffee from my porcelain cups with the gold brims
and the delicate violet flowers. I become silent and gaze at
that broom flung on the floor like the rigid corpse
of that tall, slim young grocer's boy, who, years ago,
showed me his big phallus between the railings of the garden gate.

Oh yes, I laugh sometimes, and I hear my hoarse laughter rise up,
no longer from the chest, but much deeper, from the feet; even
    deeper,
from the earth. I laugh. How pointless it all was,
how purposeless, ephemeral and insubstantial — riches, wars, glories,
jealousies, jewels, my own beauty.
                                    What foolish legends,
swans and Troys and loves and brave deeds.
                                    I met my old
lovers again in mournful night feasts, with white beards,
with white hair, with bulging bellies, as though they were
already pregnant with their death, devouring with a strange craving
the roasted goats, without looking into a shoulder-blade — what
    should they look for? —
a level shadow filled all of it with a few white specks.

I, as you know, preserved my former beauty
as if by miracle (but also with tints, herbs and salves,
lemon juice and cucumber water). I was only terrified to see
     in their faces
the passing also of my own years. At that time I was tightening
     my belly muscles,
I was tightening my cheeks with a false smile, as though
propping up two crumbling walls with a thin beam.

That's how I was, shut in, confined, strained — God, what exhaustion —
confined every moment (even in my sleep) as though I were inside
freezing armor or a wooden corset around my whole body, or within
my own Trojan Horse, deceptive and narrow, knowing even then
the pointlessness of deceit and self-deception, the pointlessness of
     fame,
the pointlessness and temporality of every victory.
                                        A few months ago,
when I lost my husband (was it months or years?), I left
my Trojan Horse forever down in the stable, with his old horses,
so the scorpions and spiders could circle around inside him. I
     don't tint my hair anymore.

Huge warts have sprouted on my face. Thick hairs have grown
     around my mouth —
I clutch them; I don't look at myself in the mirror —
long, wild hairs — as though someone else has enthroned himself
     within me,
an impudent, malevolent man, and it's his beard
that emerges from my skin. I leave him be — what can I do? —
I'm afraid that if I chased him away, he'd drag me along behind him.

Don't go away. Stay awhile longer. I haven't talked for ages.
Nobody comes to see me anymore. They were all in a hurry to leave,
I saw it in their eyes — all in a hurry for me to die. Time doesn't
     roll on.
The servants loathe me. I hear them opening my drawers at night,
taking the lacy things, the jewels, the gold coins; who can tell

if they'll leave me with a single decent dress for some necessary
    hour
or a single pair of shoes. They even took my keys
from under my pillow; I didn't stir at all; I pretended I was
    asleep —
they would have taken them one day anyway — I don't want them to know,
    at least, that I know.

What would I do without even them? 'Patience, patience,' I tell
    myself;
'patience' — and this too is the smallest form of victory,
when they read the old letters of my admirers
or the poems great poets dedicated to me; they read them
with idiotic bombast and many mistakes in pronunciation,
    accentuation, metre
and syllabification — I don't correct them. I pretend I don't hear.
    Occasionally
they draw big moustaches with my black eyebrow pencil
on my statues, or stick an ancient helmet or a chamber-pot
on their heads. I regard them coolly. They get angry.

One day, when I felt a little better, I asked them again
to make up my face. They did. I asked for a mirror.
They had painted my face green, with a black mouth. 'Thank you,'
    I told them,
as though I hadn't seen anything strange. They were laughing. One
    of them
stripped right in front of me, put on my gold veils, and like that,
bare-legged with her thick legs began to dance,
leapt upon the table — frenzied; danced and danced, bowing
in imitation, as it were, of my old gestures. High up on her thigh
she had a love-bite from a man's strong even teeth.
I watched them as though I were in the theatre — with no humiliation
    or grief,
or indignation — for what purpose? — But I kept telling myself:
'one day we'll die,' or rather: 'one day you will,' and that
was a sure revenge, fear and consolation. I looked
everything straight in the eye with an indescribable, apathetic
    clarity, as if

my eyes were independent of me; I looked at my own eyes
situated a metre away from my face, like the panes
of a window far removed, from behind which someone else
sits and observes the goings-on in an unknown street
with closed coffee, photograph and perfume shops,
and I had the feeling that a beautiful crystal phial
broke, and the perfume spilled out in the dusty showcase. Everyone
    passing,
pausing vaguely, sniffing the air, remembered something good
and then disappeared behind the pepper-trees or at the end of the
    street.

Now and again, I can still sense that aroma — I mean, I remember it;
isn't it strange? — those things we usually consider great, dissolve,
    fade away —
Agamemnon's murder, the slaughter of Clytemnestra (they'd sent me
one of her beautiful necklaces from Mycenae, made
from small gold masks, held together by links
from the upper tips of their ears — I never wore it). They're
    forgotten;
some other things remain, unimportant, meaningless things; I
    recall seeing one day
a bird perching on a horse's back; and that baffling thing
seemed to explain (especially for me) a certain beautiful mystery.

I still remember, as a child, on the banks of the Eurotas, beside
    the burning leanders,
the sound of a tree peeling off alone; the bark
falling gently into the water and floating away like triremes,
and I waited, stubbornly, for a black butterfly with orange stripes
to land on a piece of bark, amazed that although it was immobile,
    it moved,
and this broke me up, that butterflies, although adept in air,
know nothing about travelling in water, or rowing. And it came.

There are certain strange, isolated moments, almost funny. A man
takes a stroll at midday wearing a huge hamper on his head; the
    basket

hides his whole face as though he were headless or disguised
by an enormous eyeless, multi-eyed head. Another man,
strolling along, musing in the dusk, stumbles over something,
    curses,
turns back, searches — finds a pebble, picks it up; kisses it; then
remembers to look around; goes off guiltily. A woman
slips her hand inside her pocket; finds nothing; takes her hand
    out,
raises it and carefully scrutinizes it, as though it were breathed
    on by the powder of emptiness.

A waiter's caught a fly in his hand — he doesn't crush it;
a customer calls him; he's absorbed; he loosens his fist; the fly
escapes and lands on the glass. A piece of paper rolls down the
    street
hesitantly, spasmodically, attracting nobody's
attention — enjoying it all. But yet, every so often
it gives off a certain crackle which belies it; as though looking for
an impartial witness to its humble, secret route. And all these things
have a desolate and inexplicable beauty, and a profound pain
because of our own odd and unknown gestures — don't they?

The rest is lost as though it were nothing. Argos, Athens, Sparta,
Corinth, Thebes, Sikion — shadows of names. I utter them; they
    re-echo as though they're sinking
into the incomplete. A well-bred, lost dog stands
in front of the window of a cheap dairy. A young girl passing by
    looks at it;
it doesn't respond; its shadow spreads wide in the sidewalk.
I never learned the reason. I doubt it even exists. There's
    only
this humiliating compulsive (by whom?) approval
as we nod 'yes,' as though greeting someone
with incredible servility, though nobody's passing, nobody's there.

I think another person, with a totally colorless voice related to me
    one evening
the details of my life; I was sleepy and wishing deep inside

that he'd finally stop; that I could close my eyes,
and sleep. And as he spoke, in order to do something, to fight
    off sleep,
I counted the tassels on my shawl, one by one, to the tune of
a silly children's song of Blindman's Buff, until
the meaning got lost in the repetition. But the sound remains —
noises, thuds, scrapings — the drone of silence, a discordant weeping,
someone scratches the wall with his fingernails, a scissor falls
    onto the floor boards,
someone coughs — his hand over his mouth, so as not to awaken the
    other
sleeping with him — maybe his death — stops; and once again
that spiralling drone from an empty, shut-up well.

At night I hear the servants moving my big pieces of furniture;
they take them down the stairs — a mirror, held like a stretcher,
reveals the worn-out plaster designs on the ceiling; a windowpane
knocks against the railings — it doesn't break; the old overcoat on
    the coat-rack
raises its empty arms for a moment, slips them back into the pockets;
the little wheels of the sofa's legs creak on the floor. I can feel
right here on my elbow the scratching on the wall made by the corners
    of the wardrobe
or the big carved table. What are they going to do with them?
    'Goodbye,' I say
almost mechanically, as though bidding farewell to a visitor who's
    always a stranger. There's only
that vague droning which lingers in the hallway as though from the
    horn
of downfallen hunting lords in the last drops of rain, in a burnt-out-
    forest.
Honestly, so many useless things collected with so much greed
blocked the space — we couldn't move; our knees
knocked against wooden, stony, metallic knees. Oh, we've really
got to grow old, very old, to become just, to reach that
mild impartiality, that sweet lack of interest in comparisons,
    judgements,
when it's no longer our lot to take part in anything except this
    quietness.

Oh yes, how many silly battles, heroic deeds, ambitions, arrogance,
sacrifices and defeats, defeats, and still more battles for things
that others determined when we weren't there. Innocent people
poking hairpins into their eyes, banging their heads
on the high wall, knowing full well that it wouldn't fall
or even crack, just to see at least from a little crevice
a slight sky-blue unshadowed by time and their own shadows. Meanwhile —
    who knows —
perhaps there, where someone is resisting, hopelessly, perhaps there
human history begins, so to speak, and man's beauty
among rusty bits of iron and the bones of bulls and horses,
among ancient tripods where some laurel still burns
and the smoke rises curling in the sunset like a golden fleece.

Stay awhile longer. Evening's falling. The golden fleece we spoke
    of — Oh, thought
comes slowly to us women — it relaxes somehow. On the other hand
    men
never stop to think — maybe they're afraid; maybe they don't want
to look their fear straight in the eye, to see their fatigue, to
    relax —
timid, conceited, busybodies, they surge into darkness. Their
    clothes
always smell of smoke from a conflagration they've passed by or
    through
unwittingly. Quickly they undress; fling
their clothes onto the floor; fall into bed. But even their bodies
reek of smoke — it numbs them. I used to find, when they were finally
    asleep,
some fine burnt leaves among the hairs on their chests
or some ash-grey down from slain birds. Then
I'd gather them up and keep them in a small box — the only signs
of a secret communion — I never showed these to them — they wouldn't
    have recognized them.

Sometimes, oh yes, they were beautiful — naked as they were, surrendered
    to sleep,
thoroughly unresisting, loosened up, their big strong bodies,
damp and softened, like roaring rivers surging down

from high mountains into a quiet plain, or like abandoned children.
   At such times
I really loved them, as though I'd given birth to them. I noticed
   their long eyelashes
and I wanted to draw them back into me, to protect them, or in
   this way
to couple with their whole bodies. They were sleeping. And sleep
   demands respect
from you, because it's so rare. That's all over too. All forgotten.

Not that I don't remember anymore — I do; it's just that the memories
are no longer emotional — they can't move us — they're impersonal,
   placid,
clear right into their most bloody corners. Only one of them
still retains some air around it, and breathes.
                          That late afternoon,
when I was surrounded by the endless shrieks of the wounded,
the mumbled curses of the old men and their wonder of me, amid
the smell of overall death, which, from time to time glittered
on a shield or the tip of a spear or the metope
of a neglected temple or the wheel of a chariot — I went up alone
onto the high walls and strolled around.
                         alone, utterly alone, between
the Trojans and Achaeans, feeling the wind pressing my fine veils
against me, brushing my nipples, embracing my whole body
both clothed and naked, with only a single wide silver belt
holding my breasts up high —
                   there I was, beautiful, untouched, experienced
while my two rivals in love were duelling and the fate of the long war
was being determined —
              I didn't even see the strap of Paris' helmet
severed — instead I saw a brightness from its brass,
a circular brightness, as his opponent swung it in rage
around his head — an illumined zero.
                It wasn't really worth looking at —
the will of the gods had shaped things from the start; and Paris,
divested of his dusty sandals, would soon be in bed,
cleansed by the hands of the goddess, waiting for me, smirking,
pretentiously hiding a false scar on his side with a pink bandage.

I didn't watch anymore; hardly even listened to their war-cries —
I, high up on the walls, over the heads of mortals, airy, carnate,
belonging to no one, needing no one
as though I were (I, independent) absolute Love — free
from the fear of death and time, with a white flower in my hair,
with a flower between my breasts, and another in between my lips
    hiding for me
the smile of freedom.
                        They could have shot
their arrows at me from either side.
                                I was an easy target
walking slowly on the walls, completely etched
against the golden crimson of the evening sky.
                                    I kept my eyes closed
to make any hostile gesture easy for them — knowing deeply
that none of them would dare. Their hands trembled with awe
at my beauty and immortality —
                        (maybe I can elaborate on that:
I didn't fear death because I felt it was so far from me).
                                            Then
I tossed down the two flowers from my hair and breasts — keeping
    the third one
in my mouth — I tossed them down from both sides of the wall
with an absolutely impartial gesture.
                            Then the men, both within and without,
threw themselves upon each other, enemies and friends, to snatch
the flowers, to offer them to me — my own flowers. I didn't see
anything else after that — only bent backs, as if all of them
were kneeling on the ground, where the sun was drying the blood —
    maybe
they had even crushed the flowers.
                            I didn't see.
                                    I'd raised my arms
and risen on the tips of my toes, and ascended
letting the third flower also drop from my lips.

All this remains with me still — a sort of consolation, a remote
    justification, and perhaps
this will remain, I hope, somewhere in the world — a momentary freedom,

illusory too of course – a game of our luck and our ignorance. In
   precisely
that position (as I recall), the sculptors worked on
my last statues; they're still out there in the garden;
you must have seen them when you came in. Sometimes I also (when
   the servants are in good spirits
and hold me by my arms to take me to that chair
in front of the window), I also can see them. They glow in the sun-
   light. A white heat
wafts from the marble right up here. I won't dwell on it any
   longer.
It tires me out too after awhile. I'd rather watch a part of the
   street
where two or three kids play with a rag ball, or some girl
lowers a basket on a rope from the balcony across the way.
Sometimes the servants forget I'm there. They don't come to put
   me back in bed.
I stay all night gazing at an old bicycle, propped up
in front of the lit window of a new candy store,
until the lights go out, or I fall asleep on the window-sill.
   Every now
and then I think that a star wakes me, falling through space
like the saliva from a toothless, slack mouth of an old man.
                                                        Now
it's been ages since they've taken me to the window. I stay here in
   bed
sitting up or lying down – I can handle that. To pass the time
I grasp my face – an unfamiliar face – touch it, feel it, count
the hairs, the wrinkles, the warts – who's inside
this face?
            Something acrid rises in my throat – nausea and fear,
a silly fear, my God, that even the nausea might be lost. Stay
   for awhile –
a little light's coming through the window – they must have lit the
   street lamps.

Wouldn't you like me to ring for something for you? – some
   preserved cherries
or candied bitter orange – maybe something's left in the big jars,
turned to congealed sugar by now – if, of course the greedy servants

have left anything. The last few years I've been busy
making sweets — what else is there to do?

                                    After Troy — life in Sparta
was very dull — really provincial; shut up all day at home,
among the crowded spoils of so many wars; and memories,
faded and annoying, sneaking up behind you in the mirror
as you combed your hair, or in the kitchen emerging
from the greasy vapors of the pot; and you hear in the water's
    boiling
a few dactylic hexameters from the Third Rhapsody
as a cock crows discordantly, close by, from a neighbor's coop.

You surely know how humdrum our life is. Even the newspapers
have the same shape, size, headlines — I no longer read them.
    Over and over
flags on balconies, national celebrations, parades
of toy soldiers — only the cavalry maintained something improvised,
something personal — maybe because of the horses. The dust rose
    like a cloud;
we closed the window — afterward you'd have to go about dusting,
    piece by piece,
vases, little boxes, picture frames, small porcelain statues,
    mirrors, buffets.
I stopped going to the celebrations. My husband used to come
    back sweating,
fling himself on his food, licking his chops, re-chewing
old, boring glories and resentments gone up in smoke. I stared at
his waistcoat buttons which were about to pop — he'd become quite
    fat.
Under his chin a large black stain flickered.

Then I'd prop my chin up, distractedly, continuing my meal,
feeling my lower jaw move in my hand
as though it were detached from my head, and I was holding it naked
    in my palm.
Maybe because of this I got fat too. I don't know. Everybody seemed
    scared —
I saw them sometimes from the windows — walking on a slant,
sort of limping, as though they were concealing something under

their arms. Afternoons
the bells rang dismally. The beggars knocked on the doors. In the
     distance
as night fell, the white-washed facade of the Maternity Hospital
     seemed whiter,
farther away and unknowable. We lit the lamps quickly. I'd alter
an old dress. Then the sewing machine broke down; they took it
into the basement with those old romantic oil paintings
full of banal mythical scenes — Aphrodites rising from the sea,
     Eagles and Ganymedes.

One by one our old acquaintances left. The mail diminished.
Only a brief postcard for special occasions, birthdays —
a stereotyped scene of Mount Taygetos with ridged peaks, very blue,
a part of the Eurotas river with white pebbles and rhododendrons,
or the ruins of Mistras with wild fig trees. But more often,
telegrams of condolences. No answers came. Maybe
the recipient had died in the meantime — we don't get news anymore.

My husband travelled no more. Didn't open a book. In his later
     years
he grew very nervous. He smoked incessantly. Strolled around at
     nights
in the huge living room, with those tattered brown slippers
and his long nightgown. At noon, at the table, he'd bring up
     memories
of Clytemnestra's infidelity and how right Orestes' actions were
as though he were threatening someone. Who cared? I didn't even
     listen. Yet
when he died, I missed him much — I missed most of all his silly
     threats,
as though they'd frozen me into an immobile position in time,
as though they'd prevented me from becoming old.
                                        Then I used to dream
of Odysseus, he too with the same agelessness, with his smart
     triangular cap,
delaying his return, that crafty guy — with the pretence of imaginary
     dangers,
whereas he'd throw himself (supposedly ship-wrecked) at times in

the arms of a Circe, at times in the arms
of a Nausicaa, to have the barnacles taken off his chest, to be
    bathed
with small bars of rose soap, to have the scar on his knee kissed,
    to be anointed with oil.

I think he also reached Ithaca — dull, fat Penelope must have muffled
    him up
in those things she weaves. I never got a message from him since
    then —
the servants might have torn them up — what does it matter anymore?
    The Symblygades
shifted to another more inner place — you can feel them
immobile, softened — worse than ever — they don't crush,
they drown you in a thick, black fluid — nobody escapes them.
You may go now. Night's fallen. I'm sleepy. Oh, to close my eyes,
to sleep, to see nothing outside or inside, to forget
the fear of sleeping and awakening. I can't. I jump up —
I'm afraid I'll never wake again. I stay up, listening to
the snoring of the servants from the living room, the spiders on
    the walls,
the cockroaches in the kitchen, the dead snoring
with deep inhalations, as though sound asleep, calmed down.
Now I'm even losing my dead. I've lost them. They're gone.

Sometimes, after midnight, the rhythmic hoofbeats of the horses
of a late carriage can be heard, as though they are returning
from a dismal show of some broken-down theatre in the neighborhood
with its plaster fallen from the ceiling, its peeling walls,
its enormous faded red curtain drawn,
shrunken from too many washings, leaving a space below
to reveal the bare feet of the great stage manager or the electrician
maybe rolling up a paper forest so the lights can be shut off.

That crack is still alight, while in the auditorium
the applause and the chandeliers are long since vanished. The air
is heavy with the breath of silence, the hum of silence beneath
the empty seats together with the shells from sunflower seeds and

twisted-up tickets,
a few buttons, a lace handkerchief, and a piece of red string.

... And that scene, on the walls of Troy – did I really undergo an
     ascension,
letting fall from my lips – ? Sometimes even now,
as I lie here in bed, I try to raise my arms, to stand
on tiptoe – to stand on air – the third flower –

*(She stopped talking. Her head fell back. She might have been asleep. The
other person got up. He didn't say Good-night. Darkness had already come. As
he went out into the corridor, he felt the servants glued to the wall, eavesdrop-
ping. Motionless. He went down the stairs as though into a deep well, with the
feeling that he wouldn't find any exit – any door. His fingers, contracted,
searched for the doorknob. He even imagined that his hands were two birds
gasping for want of air, yet knowing at the same time that this was no more
than the expression of self-pity which we usually compare with vague fear.
Suddenly voices were heard from upstairs. The electric lights were turned on in
the corridor, on the stairs, in the rooms. He went up again. Now he was sure.
The woman was sitting on the bed with her elbow propped up on the tin table,
her cheek resting in her palm. The servants were noisily going in and out.
Somebody was making a phone call in the hall. The women in the neighborhood rushed in. 'Ah, ah,' they cried, as they hid things under their dresses.
Another phone call. Already the police were coming up. They sent the servants
and the women away, but the neighbors had time to grab the bird cages with
the canaries, some flower pots with exotic plants, a transistor, an electric heater.
One of them grabbed a gold picture frame. They put the dead woman onto a
stretcher. The person in charge sealed up the house – 'until the rightful owners
are found,' he said – although he knew there weren't any. The house would stay
like that, sealed up for forty days, and after, its possessions – as many as were
saved – would be auctioned off for the public good. 'To the morgue,' he said to
the driver. The covered car went off. Everything suddenly disappeared. Total
silence. He was alone. He turned and looked around. The moon had risen. The
statues in the garden were dimly lit – her statues, solitary, beside the trees,
outside of the closed house. And a silent, deceitful moon. Where could he go
now?).*

May-August, 1970

The Trojan Women

A PLAY BY EURIPIDES

A new version by Gwendolyn MacEwen

The Characters

HECUBA, Queen of Troy, Priam's widow. Aging, but ageless.

CASSANDRA, Hecuba's daughter, High Priestess of Apollo,
   a holy virgin. She is a nubile fifteen-year-old.

ANDROMACHE, Hector's widow. About thirty, self-righteous and shrill.

HELEN, wife of Menelaus. In her mid-twenties, beautiful,
   a pathological liar.

TALTHYBIUS, a Greek messenger.

MENELAUS, King of Sparta.

A CHORUS of nine Trojan women.

The CHILD, a boy of about five.

THE TROJAN WOMEN was first produced by Toronto Arts Productions at
The St. Lawrence Centre, Toronto, in November 1978 with the following
cast:

THE WOMEN: Diana Barrington, Jennifer Browne, Janet Doherty, Nancy
Kerr, Maxine Miller, Anna Reiser, Heather Ritchie, Ann De Villiers, and
Moira Wylie.

POSEIDON, Kenneth Pogue; HECUBA, Dawn Greenhalgh; CASSANDRA,
Diane D'Aquila; TALTHYBIUS, Kenneth Pogue; ANDROMACHE, Anne
Anglin; A BOY, Christopher Hewitt; MENELAUS, Douglas Chamberlain;
HELEN, Fiona Reid; SOLDIERS, Jay Bowen and Andrew Armstrong.

Directed by Leon Major, set and costumes designed by Murray Laufer,
lighting by Lynne Hyde, original music composed and arranged by Phil
Nimmons.

The Chorus

When not in motion, the nine women are perched upstage on the rocks which represent the broken walls of Troy. In their tattered black robes, the women resemble crows; some have tarnished jewellery.

They speak in rushed, hysterical cascades, each trying to outdo the other, butting in on one another's lines, their voices rising and falling to create an effect of sustained and relentless emotional tension. Their movements are jerky and spasmodic, creating geometric patterns which often illustrate the spoken words, e.g. 'spider's webs', 'magic circles', etc. Essentially, their role is to comment, often with sarcasm and mockery, on the weaknesses and flaws of the major characters — but in moments of tragedy they identify and sympathize with them.

The overall effect of the Chorus is impressively hideous.

Note: Each member of the Chorus is assigned a number, (1) through (9). They speak singly as indicated by the number adjacent to the line, or in chorus as indicated by (all).

Unless otherwise indicated, all entrances and exits are stage left, in the direction of the sea and the waiting Greek ships.

The Setting

The scene is set outside the broken walls of Troy. At stage right is the hut of Helen. Downstage centre there is an altar with a perpetual flame.

The play opens in the hour before dawn. The light increases by degrees, until the stage is fully lit by the time Helen appears. Helen wears a red dress slit down the back to reveal a posterior decolletage in the Spartan style.

The god Poseidon, wearing a bronze mask, is standing in front of the broken walls. The Chorus of women is sleeping on the ground.

A desolate wind blows.

POSEIDON As the moon bends the oceans
So this darkness bends the mind.
Even the planets are weary.
Everything awaits a series
    of wretched and unreal tomorrows ...

raising his voice

But *I* built these walls —
    I, Poseidon!
This city is mine,
These broken Trojan stones are mine!
And this place, this place was *Troy*
    until the Greeks came —
Until the Greeks came with their cursed Horse,
    their fabulous damned Horse,
That eased its way into my walls
With a sly and deadly form
    of magic ...

This place was Troy,
A city of sanity, of many virtues,
A queen, if I may say so, among cities!
Men were at peace with the gods,
    at peace with themselves,
    at peace with the universe ...
They worshipped the right deities
    — me, for instance —
And paid proper tribute at my shrines.
I acknowledged their tributes
By giving them no earthquakes
    for a long, long time.
They were wise, the Trojans,
They knew that only the forces of the earth
    are powerful,
    only the gods ...

Family life in Troy was flawless.
Everyone slept with whomever
They were supposed to sleep with.
It was a perfect society.

34

Women learned to sew; men learned to kill,
Honor and glory shone everywhere ...

But now, this is not Troy. Nothing rules
   here.
Spiders and grotesque insects guard the night,
The dried-up, rotten vineyards
And holy shrines that stink of blood;
Great Priam lies dead
   on some lofty stair
That supposedly leads to the altar of 'God'!

Gold, gold and gorgeous clothes
Get sent down to the ships of the Greeks.
The sailors wander on the golden beaches –
   bored and tired.
The sailors wait for the right wind
To shove them home.
(Home to women they've hardly seen
And little brats they've never known!)
Ten years ...
Ten years of sheer destruction ...

HECUBA *enters walking with a cane, followed by*
CASSANDRA. *They shuffle to the altar.*

The river moans, the air is mad
With the sounds of women – women sold
   like all the spoils of war
To foreign lords.
Even now, the Greeks are casting lots
For the best of them.

HECUBA *throws incense onto the altar, and the fire leaps up,*
revealing her face and that of CASSANDRA. CASSANDRA
wears many floral garlands and headdresses. The two women
stare into the flames, then sit on the ground and face the
audience.

The older one, the slightly wrinkled prune
   is Hecuba, queen of Troy.

Now that the king, her husband, and her
    sons are gone —

She's negotiable (like old gold).
She's both worthless and highly valuable
    (if you know what I mean).
She's nothing in terms of her body, but
Priceless because she's a queen.

She is as the city was —
Flawless, and honest, and honorable
    and clean ...

The other is little Cassandra, the
    gifted one.
She speaks in tongues. Luckily most of us
    have only one.
She's all dressed up and ready
For some lucky man's bed. Unlucky lady,
    little bride of rage ...

The light intensifies as dawn approaches.

To Hell with all of it, to Hell
    with these splendid towers,
    this once magnificent citadel,
    this horrible heap of stones!
This place, this place was Troy ...

gazing out stage left, towards the ships

Beware, you invaders!
You wear the same faces now
    that you have worn
    since the Beginning ...
But you will die, because Troy dies,
    because
Everything dies!

exits stage right

CHORUS   The dark is hungry
              just before the dawn. [1]
          It devours Troy. [2]
          The darkness is starving; it eats
              the stones. [3]
          Dawn does not come. [4]
          The gods do not come ... [5]
          God come and go ... [6]
          Gods are the fools that reside
              in our heads. [7]
          They are *nothing more*. [8]
          And nothing less.

              They slowly get up as HECUBA *walks around.*

HECUBA   Circles of darkness are like the webs
              of spiders.
          My body is a bug; I am a grotesque insect.
          I have been sleeping on the ground.
          History is a spider's web.
          This is not Troy, this
          Is not Troy!

CHORUS   History is a spider's web.
          This is not Troy. This is a perfect
              world of pain. [1]
          Time is a world of pain
          that circles 'round with stars and planets
          In the dizzy skies! [2]
          Time circles back to Genesis. [3]
          We women have learned nothing. [4]
          Time has learned nothing. [5]
          We have learned nothing. [6]
          History is a spider's web.
          The dark is hungry just before the
              dawn. [7]
          The dark is starving; it eats the stones.
          But dawn will come. [8]
          Circles of darkness are
          The dark webs of spiders. This is
              not Troy. [9]

37

The CHORUS *climb onto the rocks.*

HECUBA This is not Troy, and we no longer rule here,
Bats and lizards rule here.
Jackals eat the night. Even the wind
   is slowly going mad!
What happened, what happened?
How can this be? The centre
   drops out of the world
And it's not a dream — it's reality!
Agony survives where nothing else survives.
Nothing is alive but the hungry dark.
   If Troy is gone, then everything is gone.
   Everything I believed in, everything I
   lived for —
   Piety and honesty and honor and glory.
   Especially piety ...
      for only the forces of the earth
      are powerful, only the gods!
If Troy is meaningless then everything
Is meaningless — this tongue, these hands,
The shoddy wonders of what we call the
   spirit
And the mind ... and this cannot be so!
There must be some holy meaning
   behind this destruction.
Only the forces of the earth are powerful,
Only the *gods*!

HECUBA *goes over to the hut of Helen.*

Helen? Helen? *Helen,* are you there?

CHORUS Helen? Helen? *Helen,* are you there? *all*

laughter from the hut

HECUBA Are you afraid to come out, you useless
   bitch?
Helen, Helen, Helen, it was all your
   doing —
   this filthy war, this

unremarkable, miserable dying ...
I, Hecuba, a queen, have been reduced
    to nothing.
I'm a widow waiting for a *Greek* to claim me,
A slave for the enemy!
All the glory's wrung from me. I assume
    the shapes of rage. I'm twisted;
I'm a piece of driftwood in some anonymous sea.

pausing

Foreigners came here wearing *faces*
(in this case, Greek faces) —
Came here with their anger and their
    laughter and their sweet, wild
    flutes ...
And what did they come for, the sweet,
    wild Greeks?
They came to rescue a great king's wife,
They came to rescue a slut from Sparta.
They came for *Helen,* evil child!

gazing at CASSANDRA

Thank heaven *my child* is pure and clean,
My little holy virgin, Apollo's bride,
High Priestess of the god,
Sweet little Cassandra ...

HECUBA *returns to the altar.* CASSANDRA *gets up, turns, and
looks at the* CHORUS. *She laughs.*

CASSANDRA Oh, let's sing some *new* songs, —
            Not the ones we used to sing when
                the gods were listening,
            But *new* songs, like ...

    CHORUS Helen, Helen, *Helen,* are you there? *all*

CASSANDRA Not *that* one!
            Well come on down, you pitiful things,
                you old black crows!

Why don't you join me, you black brides?
We'll weep for Troy, a dying fire, yet —
an everlasting flame!

HECUBA Come down from your rocks, you ugly ducklings!
Black birds, black brides,
you stinky things!

Some members of the CHORUS *hesitantly come down.*

I've got something to tell you …
The time has come, the time we've all been waiting for!
Do you hear, do you hear?
The Greeks in the ships down at the shore
Are getting up and moving around …
The time for our departure is drawing near,
Yes, the time is drawing near!

CHORUS *wailing*
How far will they take me, how far away? [4]
A foreign life, a foreign land! [5]
In an enemy's bed, an enemy's bed! [6]

CASSANDRA Stop wailing! Why are you so *stupid*!
When I go, I go willingly, yes, *willingly*
Down to the ships of the Greeks, down
to the shore.
Have you learned nothing from this war?

pauses

Nothing is destroyed that is not ripe
for destruction.
Troy was ripe for it. Troy was destroyed!

HECUBA *gasps at this. Two members of the* CHORUS *lead*
CASSANDRA *away from her.*

CHORUS Leave her alone, she's mad … [7]
Leave her alone, she's mad … [8]
Leave her alone, she's mad … [9]
I dreamt I slept

With a Greek king, in a Greek
    king's bed. [1]
I wish they'd kill me, I'd rather
    be dead! [2]
I'm dying of fear, I'm dying ... [3]
It is only morning ... [4]

It's only morning, and yet they're
    coming! [5]
Which one will take me? I'm not
    ready! [6]
They'll take me to Argos, or maybe
Some naked lonely island far far
    away ... [7]
I will continue to weave,
But on somebody else's loom ... [8]
I will carry pitchers of water,
    pitchers of water,
I will carry pitchers of water
From one end of the earth to the other
Forever and ever ... [9]

HECUBA *screaming*
What about me? I look like death,
Like the stones carved for a dead
    man's grave.
Will they make me take care of my
    enemy's children,
Or open my enemy's door?
I was Queen of Troy!

CHORUS Shame, shame, shame ... *all*
A Greek's bed in the night ... [2]
Slaves, slaves, slaves ... [3]
We are all slaves ... *all*

CASSANDRA Sssh!
The messenger is coming!

TALTHYBIUS *enters with one soldier.*

TALTHYBIUS Greetings, Hecuba.

You already know me.
I bring, as always, messages from the
Greeks.

HECUBA Go to Hell, Talthybius.

CHORUS The waiting's over, sisters! [5]
The bidding's over! [6]
Who gets us? Where do we go? [7]
It might be Thebes. [8]
It might be Thessaly. [9]

HECUBA The place, ladies, is called Nowhere.

TALTHYBIUS You're not all going together like cows,
I mean, not as a herd. I mean,
You'll all be leaving separately.

CASSANDRA *approaches* TALTHYBIUS *and strokes his face.*

CASSANDRA Who gets me? Who gets Cassandra?

TALTHYBIUS The great Agamemnon himself!
Is that not an honor, is that not glory?

CASSANDRA *becoming even more flirtatious*
Generous words, you gentle enemy ...
Tell me, what will the great Agamemnon
Make me do?
I wonder, I wonder ...
Will I wash dishes for his wife?
Will I be the servant of Helen's sister?

TALTHYBIUS I think you know what he'll make you do.

HECUBA Leave her alone! She's a holy child!
She's a sacred virgin, the Beloved of Apollo!

TALTHYBIUS That's why the king wants her.
It makes it that much more interesting ...

HECUBA *to* CASSANDRA *as she leads her to the altar*
Don't be alarmed, child.
Keep repeating to yourself —
men are fools, men are fools.
We live in a world of men,
We live beneath their shadows.
But without them we are nothing.
Know this.
Please be proud, and honorable.

CASSANDRA *laughing and casting off her black cloak
to reveal a transparent white gown*
Oh, mother! Can't you see that I'm
laughing
Because it's all so *funny*?

CASSANDRA *takes a torch and lights it at the altar, then swings
it around gleefully.*

TALTHYBIUS Stop her — she'll burn the whole place
down!
I have to answer to the *king*!

HECUBA It's all right. She's the child of God,
and she's quite mad. Leave her alone.

CHORUS Leave her alone, she's mad. *all*
Is she, is she? ²
Leave her alone, she's mad. *all*
Is she, is she? ⁴

CASSANDRA It's true that once I used to speak
With the awful voice of my awful Lord.
I held this fire for my God; I adored
Him, I *adored* Him!
But now I light this place, this place is lit
With every conceivable color of Heaven
and of Hell!
And when the golden voice inside my skull
Informs me of the future, gentlemen,
It tells no lies, because

43

it knows no lies to tell ...

She struts around the stage, teasing TALTHYBIUS *and soldier
with her voluptuous movements.*

What good are the gods to us now,
　　I ask you?
Did they stop this disgusting war?
Did they stop you silly boys
From running each other through
　　with your silly swords?
Did they stop the heads from rolling
　　in the bloody fields and valleys,
The mutilated hands and feet and cocks
　　being scattered and strewn
On the ground as on the floors of an
　　abattoir?
What good are the gods?

HECUBA *in a shocked whisper*
　　Cassandra, stop it!

CASSANDRA What do I care for the gods?
My breasts hurt, my groin burns
　　with another kind of fire ...
I will be a bride! I will sleep
With a real king, in a real *king's* bed!
Look then – this is the torch
Of my fabulous wedding night!
Agamemnon will run me through again and again
　　with his marvellous spear
And I will not die.
It's not *that* kind of spear, you see,
It's not *that* kind of war ...

*She caresses the torch, treating it as a phallus, then throws
herself against the soldier, laughing. Breaking away from his
restraining arm, she runs to the opposite side of the stage.*

Fire out of the mouths of the gods,
Fire out of the loins of men,

Wonderful fire!
I'm a holy virgin about to be wed.
Do you like my wedding dress, mother?
Maybe you think it's a bit too sexy
    for a bride.
I thought I was *supposed* to be
    a sexy bride!

HECUBA *makes an angry lunge at* CASSANDRA. *Two women*
of the CHORUS *hold her back.* TALTHYBIUS *grabs the torch*
and extinguishes it against the ground.

HECUBA   Why, why, *why*, Cassandra?

CASSANDRA   I am young. Life is short.
This war has shown me all I ever need to see
Of the outcome of piety and honor,
    the 'good' society.

CHORUS   But what else is there? [1]
Chaos? [2]
Anarchy? [3]

HECUBA   You are the bride of Apollo,
A holy child.
You cannot go to the bed of the
    enemy willingly —
Scream, at least! Curse your fate!
Cassandra!

CASSANDRA   I curse the smug self-righteous stones
Which are the foundation of this city!
I curse the smug, self-righteous rules
We were supposed to live by.
I curse these causes of a war
Which is the same war forever,
    fought over and over
In all the bloody fields of history!

CHORUS   She does not curse her Fate … [4]
Because there is no 'Fate' to curse. [5]
She does not blame the gods [6]

45

Because there are no 'gods' to blame. [7]
What does she blame, then, what does
    she curse? [8]
All of us, all of us ... *all*

CASSANDRA *going to the hut of* HELEN *and pausing outside*
What's the difference between holy and
    unholy fire?
Look, I'll make magic circles with
    my wondrous music.
Am I not, then, as sexy as Helen,
As desirable as the *sunrise*?

*On the last word, a flute sounds, so distant and thin that it's
almost imaginary.* CASSANDRA *dances a dance of spiritual
and sexual liberation. At the end, she falls to the ground and
writhes around in what might be an orgasm, a 'holy
possession' or an epileptic fit.*

CHORUS *huddling over her*
She's the child of God. [1]
Leave her alone, she's mad. [2]
Leave her alone, she's mad. [3]
Or is she? [4]
Or *is* she? [5]

CHORUS *disperses.*

Silly little bitch. [6]
There was a time when fire was holy ... [7]
Red flames on birth-nights ... [8]
Torches for somebody's death-day ... [9]
Who among us ever dreamed of war? [1]
Scarlet swords, *death's* birthday! [2]
Nothing is holy anymore. [3]
Fire is not holy. [4]
Fire is only fire. [5]

CASSANDRA *slowly getting up and addressing* TALTHYBIUS
You fell by the thousands, you poor fools,
And all because of a whore called Helen,
    or whatever she embodied,

whatever she stood for,
   whatever smug, self-righteous rules
She had to live by.
And for her ridiculous husband,
   the mighty invincible cuckold,
   Menelaus,
You fought here on our shores,
   you miserable children,
   and you died.

CHORUS   Troy dies. [1]
Everything dies. [2]
Everything dies but *Death*. [3]

CASSANDRA   Poor warrior, miserable child ...
How long have you been here in Troy?
Do you have any children of your own?
You don't know. Of course not.
Even if you had, you'd never have seen them ...

caressing TALTHYBIUS

Absurd wars create absurd heroes,
All wars are absurd; therefore
   all heroes are absurd.
And all this filthy nonsense
   will go down in history!
Is that not so, Talthybius?
There are no good guys and no bad guys.
Just all you silly little soldiers.

TALTHYBIUS   *grabbing her arm*
You've exhausted my patience, witch.
Come on!

CASSANDRA   *wrenching herself away*
I know the places where the unofficial
   future lies —
I know the dark, dark places where
   secrets scream to be laid bare.
But I will say no more because I know
   too much.

47

I know a lot of your secrets, soldier.
O, wouldn't you like to lay *me* bare?
Am I not as sexy as Helen,
As desirable as the sunrise?

CHORUS   What is as short-lived
        as the sunrise? ⁴

CASSANDRA   *tearing off her floral garlands*
Flowers, flowers, holy flowers,
Flowers of my god, O marvellous flowers …
Flowers, flowers, flowers in my hair!
I've forgotten what you mean,
    so I'll throw you all away!

*Suddenly her voice becomes a terrified whisper, and she gazes
out over the audience as though in a trance.*

The golden voice of the god was in
    my head for the last time.
Pictures of the future came leaping
    through the flames.
I did not like what I had to see —
Other wars for other insane reasons,
A repetition of history.
    Agamemnon, you die.
    You are snuffed out
Like all miserable ephemeral things
    that burn and glow and breathe
    and scream.

You die in darkness. I see your end.
I see you cushioned within hills
Made silver-grey with icy rain.
    You are stark dead; you are stark
    naked
Like a giant snail wrenched from its shell.
I am there with you.
I am naked and abandoned …
Oh! The jackals and the jackals
    and more jackals
    circle 'round!…

48

CHORUS The jackals [5]
And the jackals [7]
And more jackals circle 'round. [8]

CASSANDRA *shaking herself back to normal*
Never mind all that, Cassandra!
Take me to the ship then, soldier.
The wind's rising.
One of the Furies is with me now,
    one of the sisters of Hell.
Goodbye, mother – goodbye, city!
I'm glad to leave, I'm glad of it!

She addresses HECUBA, *who refuses to turn from the altar.*

Mother, I know you would like to see
The destruction of your enemies.
You would like me to return radiant
    from the wreck of the house of Atreus.
You would like me to burn it all down,
    wouldn't you?

But I have no enemies.
I believe everything and nothing.
I am fire.

HECUBA You *harlot*!

CASSANDRA *is led out, laughing.*

CHORUS The jackals and the jackals and more jackals
    circle 'round ... [6]
She's mad, she's mad! [7]

laughing

She's a child of God! [8]

laughing

Is she really, is she really? [9]

CHORUS   What does she have to lose anyway? [4]
         The same thing we lost years ago, ladies —
         Our *holy virginity*! [5]

HECUBA   I never *knew* her!
         The little flirt, the little fool ...
         I never knew she used her body
             to bend men to her will.

CHORUS   She knows the places where the unofficial
             future lies ... [1]
         The dark, dark places where secrets scream
             to be laid bare ... [2]
         Is she mad or is she not? [3]
         Is she holy or is she not? [4]

HECUBA   *I do not care!*
         I never knew her gift for prophecy was a tool
         She used to manipulate and shape her world.
         I do not care if she's demonic or divine,
         If she's a child of Heaven or of Hell —
             she's *mine*!

         She sobs briefly, then forces her attention towards
         TALTHYBIUS.

         What about me? Whose slave will I be?
         Me with my grotesque body, the body
         Of a bug that's slept on the ground?
         Me with my skinny, flailing arms?
             my interesting arthritis,
             my queenly limbs all wrapped around
         This *stunning* cane? Eh, eh? Who gets
         My *soul*, Talthybius, my useless appendages,
             my selves.
         All hanging out, all dangling
         Around this prop, this golden crutch?...

TALTHYBIUS   Ulysses, the king of Ithaca, is *mad* about you!

HECUBA *trying unsuccessfully to swat him with her cane*
Ulysses is an animal.

TALTHYBIUS He is a great king.

HECUBA Ulysses is a disgusting, horny animal!
I know what I look like,
I'm as old as the mountains, older maybe.
I'm as old as a fairy tale or a dirty joke.
    I'm almost as old as the sea.

strutting around grotesquely

I know this Ulysses, I know what he wants! Ladies —
He's only after me for my *body*!

HECUBA *and the* CHORUS *roar with laughter.* HECUBA *struts
around some more, then trips and falls in a heap on the
ground.* TALTHYBIUS *pauses, shrugs, and exits. A member of
the* CHORUS *comes down and helps* HECUBA *up.*

O leave me alone, don't fuss over me.
Do you think that after all that's happened,
This ruined body can't take a little fall?

She gets up with difficulty.

Should I call upon the gods,
The gods who dwell in circles of darkness,
Who make mighty rules
    and follow none,
    the golden lords who live
    above the law?...

Should I lean on the gods as I lean on
    this cane
Because something in me still cries out? —
The terrified child who lives in the mind,
the original, phantom self which drowns
    in the lungs —
Cries out: God, God, *God*!

Cries out like a drowning man in a sea
    with no bottom,
Cries out like the soul on the beaches
    of Nowhere.
        ... or like a great city
        that falls, a shadow
        on the threshold of Nowhere ...

I want to call upon the gods ...
I still believe ...

But I saw my man, my king, my Lord,
    my master
Fall like a broken animal upon the holy altar,
    and I have met with men who saw my sons,
    those glorious princes, those birds
    of Troy
Quiver and shriek and vomit and die ...
How can I call upon the gods these days,
How can I pray?

Everything falls apart
In the hour before the dawn.
    Trees scatter meaningless leaves to
    the wind,
    Dreams scatter hopes, or lies.
Truth is as short-lived as the sunrise ...

Everything's coming to a close
Before it's even begun.
    I am coming to a close,
    I see my end ...
I'm an ugly old slave
Shuffling back and forth
Between here and Nowhere,
    shuffling back and forth
    among my enemies.
I open and close my enemies' doors,
I greet their guests.
    (*I,* who bore *Hector*!)
I grind their grain, I sleep on stones.
    (*I,* who slept in a royal bed!)

I wear rags against my royal flesh –
and *why*?

becoming hysterical

Because one man decided to enjoy one woman!
Helen!

CHORUS   Helen, Helen, *Helen,* are you there? *all*

HECUBA   Throw me on the earth with a rock for a
      pillow!
Let me die weeping, women of Troy!
I once walked with my head held high!
Don't believe it if any man is said to be
      happy.
Don't believe it until the day that he dies ...

The wind rises and circles around like a sudden cyclone. The
CHORUS *comes down from the rocks and begins to dance.*

CHORUS   I call upon the wind to help us make a song
      about the fall of Troy! [1]
Greek wheels bore down upon me.
I was the very earth; the hooves of a
      huge horse
Pounded against my breast ... [2]
There was this giant stallion
      with golden reins ... [3]
Gold outside, but inside, –
      fiendish steel! [4]
We went down to the gates of the city
To stare at the great beast
      of steel and gold ... [5]
It was a peace offering, they said,
A gift for Athena ... [6]
Athena, who spares no one! [7]
Inside the guts of the beast
The Greeks, like maggots, swarmed. [8]

They begin pulling a huge invisible rope.

53

They brought the Thing up through the gates.
It was like some horrible dark ship of death
    hauled up upon a beach by cables ... [9]
They brought it in front of
    the throne of Athena ... [1]
All night there was crazy music and
    dancing! [2]
All night the lamps burned like crazy,
    dancing dreams! [3]
O see the magic circles
    you can make with your fire! [4]
There was a time when fire was holy ... [5]
I danced for all the gods I knew, –
    I praised their beauty! [6]
Then, out of the steaming, sweating
    darkness,
A single *scream*! [7]
Silence fell. Silence fell like rain [8]
The only sound was the whimpering
    of a child ... [9]

The wind dies down.

Then they came out of their hiding place,
Out of the guts of the horse ... [1]
The invaders who wear the same faces now
As they wore in the Beginning ... [2]
The blood ran thick as honey
Through the streets, upon the
    thresholds ... [3]
Blood was bright wine upon the
    altars ... [4]
Troy dies, everything dies! *all*
In the darkness we stumbled
    over bodies without heads ... [6]
In the god-damned ruthless dark
We encountered Death, –
    idiotic, mindless enemy! [7]
Troy dies, everything dies! [8]
Everything dies but *Death*! [9]

There is a long silence as the CHORUS *re-assembles itself upon the rocks,* ANDROMACHE *enters, holding her son by the hand. Two soldiers accompany them.*

ANDROMACHE *in a trance*
　　　Sing for the great city that falls like
　　　　a shadow on the threshold
　　　　of Nowhere ...

HECUBA　Andromache, is it you?

ANDROMACHE　Sing for the great city that falls
　　　　like a shadow on the threshold
　　　　of Nowhere,
　　　For the hands of flame that call
　　　　all reason down,
　　　And lower babies from the cradles of the sky, —
　　　　sing for Troy!

HECUBA　*Andromache?*

ANDROMACHE　Sing for the city that descends like a dream,
　　　　the aftermath of flame ...

HECUBA　*Andromache!*

ANDROMACHE　*dully*
　　　Yes, it's I, driven forth like a cow ...
　　　My son and I have been driven
　　　　through herds of stolen cattle.
　　　The moans of the beasts
　　　　have driven us mad ...
　　　Haven't they, darling, haven't they?

The boy rushes into HECUBA's *arms.*

HECUBA　Oh, no more, *no more*!
　　　Come, child, there's nothing to fear
　　　But Fear ...

CHORUS　There's nothing to fear but Fear. [1]
　　　Did you hear? Did you hear? [2]

ANDROMACHE　There's *everything* to fear
　　　　　　　As long as you're whole and horribly alive,
　　　　　　　As long as your heart keeps pumping
　　　　　　　　　your stubborn blood through your silly veins.
　　　　　　　As long as your memory feeds on scenes
　　　　　　　　　of better times ...

　　　　　　　pausing

　　　　　　　Hector — my husband, my life!

HECUBA　Go on and weep, woman. Somehow it becomes you.
　　　　　But you're not the only one to lose your man.
　　　　　God willing, this is the end, this is
　　　　　　　the war to end all wars ...

ANDROMACHE　*God willing?* God doesn't know you, Hecuba.
　　　　　　　God doesn't know *me*! Which god? Does it matter?

HECUBA　You sound just like Cassandra.
　　　　　You, Andromache!
　　　　　Do you also mock the gods?

ANDROMACHE　What are the gods to me?
　　　　　　　Small or great, what are they to *me*?
　　　　　　　I'm a *woman*.
　　　　　　　I know all about the depths of suffering,
　　　　　　　Great yawning chasms of pain
　　　　　　　　　like black cavities in the earth
　　　　　　　　　or the guts of volcanoes
　　　　　　　That open up to reveal
　　　　　　　The fathomless mouths of the fathomless 'gods'
　　　　　　　Which are nothing but our fears and desires
　　　　　　　　　made huge and horrible,
　　　　　　　　　spewing forth blood, and lava.
　　　　　　　There is no bottom to those craters ...
　　　　　　　There is no end to pain ...

CHORUS　The soul is a shattered landscape,
　　　　　　　a once-fabulous country
　　　　　Wrenched apart by a sudden earthquake. [7]
　　　　　The rift does not heal. [8]

56

The giant wound does not heal.
It bleeds poison, liquid fire ... [9]

ANDROMACHE Hector – my husband, my *life*!

HECUBA O stop it! Did you have no life of your own?
He came out of me, he was *my* flesh,
But his life was his life
And his death is his death!

ANDROMACHE Now I have only the child ...

HECUBA His life, remember, is *his* life ...

ANDROMACHE Mother of so many evils, mother of pain.
You had another son whose name was Paris,
And whose black romance destroyed Troy!

CHORUS Dead men lie naked under the eyes of
Athena [1]
And all the vultures squawk for joy ... [2]

ANDROMACHE We have all suffered, it is true.
But I have suffered, old woman.
More, much more than you!

HECUBA *chuckling ironically*
Yes, oh yes. Say your say, Andromache.
It doesn't matter anymore.
We will leave this city behind –
A dried-up, desolate mother,
The echo of a desperate song, of rain,
something
That is born and dies, weeping ....

ANDROMACHE *taking the child from her, possessively*
Is that all?
Is that the future?

HECUBA *very softly*
I see the hand of God dragging the mighty down,
Bringing fools and princes, and even women

to their knees!
It is a necessary deed, horrible with logic.
It is as ruthless as a dream.
It is the hand of history, of terrible reason.
It moves swiftly, it destroys
    all that we might have become,
    all that we have ever been ...

ANDROMACHE I don't understand!
Why can't we just die then!
You awful old witch with your awful vision!
Why can't we just lie down and *die*!
Why must we stand here like fools and *scream*!

CHORUS Why must we stand here like fools and *scream*! *all*

HECUBA You're wrong. Death is utter emptiness.
In life there is always hope ...

ANDROMACHE No, no, no! Death is just *not-being*
And why should we bother to *be*
    In a world of perpetual pain?
The dead do not suffer, or wallow in misery ...
I think they are more like funny embryos,
    like unborn babies, — do you see?
They float, they float, in a state of
Meaningless but interesting ecstasy ...
But the living! Ha! Fools, fools
    with horrible hungers,
    lost, lost before they even come to be!

The dead don't care about life, I know it.
But I — and I am the living — I want
    the *best* of all things! I swear it.
Because of this, I will never know peace,
    I will never be free.

CHORUS The dead know nothing of life! [1]
The dead don't care about life! [2]
That's what she said. [3]
She means it. [4]

ANDROMACHE

Suddenly angered, moving away from the altar to address the
CHORUS *defiantly*

I wanted the best of all things, and I *got* it!
Because of this I will never know peace.

CHORUS   She will never know peace. [5]
She means it. [6]

ANDROMACHE   *stiffening*
I was a *perfect wife*! I was perfect
for Hector's sake.
There is nothing wrong with being perfect.
In fact there is everything right with
being *perfect*.
I curbed myself, I never gave in
to the least of my whims.
I stayed at home; I had few friends.
I took care of the house; I knew my place.
I knew when to guide my man
and when to obey...

CHORUS   She took care of the house;
she knew her place. [7]
She knew when to guide and when
to obey. [8]
She was perfect, she was absolutely
perfect. [9]

ANDROMACHE   *passing by the hut of* HELEN, *pausing coyly*
The Greeks must have heard about
my virtuous behaviour...
The son of Achilles chose me immediately.
I guess he wants to have an ideal wife...
What do you think of *that*, Helen?

She waits for a reply from HELEN; *there is none.*

CHORUS   Helen, Helen, Helen are you there?... *all*

ANDROMACHE *sighing*

I don't know how to *do* it, Hecuba ...
When they carry me off to serve
    my husband's murderer.
I will not know what to do ...
I will not know what to do
When I lie there, stripped on an alien bed,
Naked as a sacrifice,
And my dead husband's enemy
    prepares to take me ...
I will not know what to do
When the son of Achilles hovers above me ...
Will I cringe, will I scream,
   Will I sing for Troy?
Before Hector took me from my father's house,
No man had ever known me.
What will I do, old woman? Tell me!

HECUBA *laughing*

Oh I'm sure you'll think of *something*,
   Andromache!
Or will you?

Men are beautiful, predictable, utter fools.
They believe, because they must believe
That a single night in their blessed bed
Will turn a normal healthy woman
   into their eternal slave!

But what woman who's known what it's *really*
   like can fake it, Andromache?
Oh, you can lie there with your knees
   pointing to heaven
Like the wings of a pale and broken bird —
But nothing will fly — neither your soul
   nor your body.
So I suggest you lie there and pretend
   you are a rock.
Men find it humiliating trying to get into
   a woman who's being a rock.

pausing and remarking wryly to herself

On the other hand, it's been so long for me
That I may not know what I'm talking about ...

ANDROMACHE I just can't stand the thought of this!
I can't adjust;
I have *principles* ...

HECUBA Oh, your virtues begin to sicken me!
Did you ever possess your *self*, Andromache?
Did you live with Hector, or *through* Hector?
I wonder, I really wonder ...
You 'perfect' wife, you suffocating mother ...

ANDROMACHE *clutching the child*
My child will grow up
To be the savior of this city!
The child of Hector – the rebuilder of Troy!
He will emerge from the midst of our enemies!
This is his destiny, this is our victory!

HECUBA *impatiently*
I think of the ships down there in the harbor.
When storms come, the sailors grab the tillers,
    man the masts, bail out of the hulls.
And when the storm's too powerful, then
    the ships give over.
They give in to Fate, they give in to the waters.
I'm like them; I have learned
    the discipline of surrender.
I no longer wonder
If anything will ever change for the better
I am a ship; I ride on the waves.
I am one with the churning waters ...

TALTHYBIUS *enters in an agony of indecision. He stutters.*

HECUBA Now what, or should I dare to wonder?

TALTHYBIUS The people and the king have decided ...
That is, the king and the people have
    decided *that* ...

ANDROMACHE *excessively confident*
That *what* — you silly, semi-plausible excuse
    for a man?
You tin soldier, you fool on the threshold
    of Nowhere, — *what*?
The king and the people have decided that ...
My son shall not go with me ... right?

TALTHYBIUS You son will not go with you.
Your son is not going ... anywhere.

CHORUS Sing for the great city that falls
    like a shadow [6]
On the threshold of Nowhere ... [7]
Your son will not go with you. [8]
Your son is not going ... anywhere. [9]

ANDROMACHE Then ... no one in Greece will be his master?

TALTHYBIUS No one in Greece will be his master ...

ANDROMACHE Then who will take care of him?

TALTHYBIUS No one.

ANDROMACHE *rhythmically rocks the child back and forth.*
Her face freezes into a smiling mask.

ANDROMACHE This is not real, because
Life is not real, because
All of this is impossible.
If it were possible,
It would be real.
But it is not real.
And so, it is *impossible*!

CHORUS History is a spider's web. [4]
The darkness devours Troy. [5]
The darkness is hungry;
    it eats the stones. [6]
Time has learned nothing, [1]

We have learned nothing. [2]
You have learned nothing! [3]

ANDROMACHE   *Stop it, stop it, stop it!*

She encircles the child in her cloak.

TALTHYBIUS   Ulysses had the final say. He said:
the son of a worthy enemy,
a glorious and therefore highly dangerous
enemy ... should not, as it were,
Grow up!

The CHORUS *leaps down and forms a human barricade
between* ANDROMACHE *and the child, and* TALTHYBIUS.

TALTHYBIUS   *his voice hollow, as though reciting something*
He shall be thrown from the walls
Onto the rocks.
It will be quick and easy. I
will make it easy ...
I will see that it is done ...

The CHORUS *raises its arms, and the black robes form what
seems to be a solid wall.* TALTHYBIUS *and the soldiers, swords
unsheathed, move forward.*

Accept it, woman! Be brave, be brave!
Look around ... there's no help anywhere!
You can't fight us. You've lost everything.
You know it. Come to your senses
for your own sake,
for your *own* sake ...

CHORUS   Sing for the great city that falls like
a shadow on the threshold of
Nowhere ... [1]
For the hands of flame that call all
reason down ... [2]
And lower babies from the cradles
of the sky! [3]
Sing for Troy! *all*

TALTHYBIUS *screaming*
　　　　　　　Stop pretending to be so goddamn *strong*!

CHORUS 　　Sing for the city that descends like
　　　　　　　　a dream, ⁵
　　　　　　　The aftermath of flame ... ⁶

TALTHYBIUS If you make a scene, it will go bad for you.
　　　　　　　Remember, just remember ...
　　　　　　　If you make a scene or protest in any way
　　　　　　　The child will have *no burial*!
　　　　　　　Do you want to see him lying
　　　　　　　　mother-naked on the rocks
　　　　　　　Shrivelled up like a pink worm, like a snail?

CHORUS 　　No burial, no burial, no burial ... ⁷ ⁸ ⁹

　　　　　　　CHORUS *disperses.*

TALTHYBIUS Give over, Andromache, and I promise
　　　　　　　The Greeks will go easy on you ...

ANDROMACHE He's all I have!
　　　　　　　I can't live without him!

HECUBA 　　And even his death is, first of all, *your* loss,
　　　　　　　You selfish woman! You parasite, you so depend
　　　　　　　　on him
　　　　　　　That even if he were to live it must be to live
　　　　　　　　for you as Hector did.
　　　　　　　You do not love, you suffocate,
　　　　　　　As you're suffocating him now beneath your skirts.
　　　　　　　Remember what I told you of my son, Hector.
　　　　　　　He came out of me, he was my flesh,
　　　　　　　But his life was *his* life
　　　　　　　And his death is *his* death!

　　　　　　　ANDROMACHE, *with an enormous effort of will, stands the*
　　　　　　　child in front of her, smooths his hair and straightens his
　　　　　　　clothes.

ANDROMACHE You're going on a journey,

You funny little thing! And where you're going
Is somewhere you've *never* been!
  It's somewhere very high —
It's where lightning falls
From the hollows of the sky!
It's higher than Troy! *Imagine!*
  And when you go,
    you'll meet your father
    with his great flashing spear
    and his deep booming laughter!
Do you remember? Do you remember?
His great flashing spear
And his deep booming laughter?

clutching the child in a violent embrace

You funny thing … you smell so nice!
Here, let's pull your cloak up,
  up around your … neck.
Give me a kiss … come on!

The child kisses ANDROMACHE, *then runs in happy*
anticipation into the arms of TALTHYBIUS, *waving his small*
sword.

TALTHYBIUS Take my hand, son.
  Let's go up to the tower!
  See — way up there above the walls!…

TALTHYBIUS *exits, stage right, with the child.*

HECUBA *running after them*
  O, you've outdone yourselves, you gentle Greeks!
  Let it be written in years to come
  That the glorious Greeks were afraid
    of a *child*!

shouting in the direction of HELEN'*s hut*

Do you hear me, Helen, daughter of Zeus
You filthy bitch, you animal?

The Greeks have surpassed themselves.
They are afraid of a *child*!

HELEN's *laughter can be heard from inside the hut.*

ANDROMACHE I am destroyed.
This is my absolute destruction.
I have nothing now. I *am* nothing.
Look, I am zero. I don't exist.
I don't exist.
Can you see me? No. I'm invisible!

She breaks out into hysterical laughter.

The soldiers lead ANDROMACHE *out.*

HECUBA *sinking to the ground beside the altar*
You exist, woman.
And what's more, you will probably survive this,
Even this ...

How can I judge her?
I also lived through men.
I had no existence apart from them.
I had a name and I had a role in life.
My name was Hecuba and my role was that
    of a queen.
I was a thing that writhed in bed
And suckled sons
And wore gold bracelets
and kept a golden, dignified silence
In the presence of men.
When my lord and my sons were killed
I too was nothing.
It was as though I had never been.

CHORUS Who were you, lady, and who are you now? [1]

HECUBA I do not know, I do not know.

The CHORUS *turn their heads and freeze, blending with the scenery.* HECUBA *hides her head in her arms, half-asleep. The morning light intensifies.* MENELAUS *enters in a great hurry, looking back to make sure that for the moment he is alone.*

MENELAUS What should I say? How can I talk to her?
I – Menelaus?

practising his speech for HELEN, *strutting back and forth pompously*

Well, Helen, my pretty ...

trying another approach

Listen, slut!
I can kill you, or enjoy you, or both.
Depending on my whim ...

He practises various macho positions.

You wonder why I'm late getting here, eh?
Ha ha *ha*!

adjusting his helmet, etc.

Do you think I had time to think of *you*
Back in Sparta?
I was busy, Helen, *busy*!
Women of many nations and many smells
And many talents
Clutched my thighs and wept
And begged me to lay them.
I was in *bed,* Helen, all the time you
    were away!
(Except when I was busy making war.)
Ha ha *ha*!

One by one the CHORUS *turn around revealing their grinning white faces.* MENELAUS *fumes with embarrassment.*

CHORUS Where's Helen, where's Helen, where's Helen? *all*

MENELAUS *to* HECUBA
Tell me, old woman, where my wife is!
The time has come. I've come to collect her.

Actually I came to get Paris.
But he's dead, so that takes care of that.

MENELAUS' *soldier enters, and* MENELAUS *kicks* HECUBA *to show his manliness in front of one of his men.*

Out with it, you old crone! Where's my wife? Where's Helen?

HECUBA *slowly gets up, turns to face him, and spits in his face.*

MENELAUS *studying her*
You spit well.
You must have been a queen,
It shows, it always shows ...
Yes, I'm sure of it ... you were a queen.
You must have been Hecuba!

HECUBA I *am* Hecuba, you dreary excuse for a man.
And I know who *you* are.

MENELAUS Of course you do. That's because I am famous.
I am a king. That's how I could tell
    that you're a queen.
They say it *shows,* you know ... royalty, I mean.
No matter what you wear, glorious robes or rags,
It shows, it always shows ...

HECUBA, *with a swift movement, grabs his helmet, revealing his advanced state of baldness.*

CHORUS *screaming with laughter*
It always shows! *all*

MENELAUS *grabs the helmet possessively.*

MENELAUS What did you do that for, you miserable bitch?

HECUBA To see what Helen's husband, the conqueror of Troy
Really looks like. Now I know. You're smooth
and round and
Bald as a baby's bum.

MENELAUS I don't want to fight with you.
I want to talk about Helen.
I want to decide what to do with her.
Should I kill her, or enjoy, or both?
I mean, she's still my wife you know ...

HECUBA *bursts out into peals of laughter.*

MENELAUS *screaming*
What's so funny? I'm serious, I'm dead serious!
Should I take her back home and have her
   killed there, or, should I do it here?
All I want is your *advice* ...
I mean, there's no point doing it here, is there?
I mean, couldn't I have her first, and kill
   her later?
Stop laughing, stop *laughing*!!

The CHORUS *also begins to laugh. There is laughter from the
hut of* HELEN.

MENELAUS *to his soldier pointing to the hut of* HELEN
Go inside there, and get her.
But let's have no violence!

The soldier enters the hut of HELEN. *From within the hut,
there comes a series of screams and giggles.*

CHORUS *playfully beating one another and
pulling one another's hair*
We are against violence! [1]
Let's have no violence *here*! [2]
After all, this is Troy! [3]
And we have no violence in *Troy*! [4]

The CHORUS *calms down. The hut is silent.*

HECUBA   Take care, Menelaus.
        Take care, 'king'.
        Your wife is evil —
          more evil than most of us dare to be,
        Because she knows nothing and she knows
          everything.
        Because she's one of the terrifying eternal
          children who think that the universe
          was created for their pleasure.
        I know her. She's a sick liar.

        Take care, Menelaus.

        Take care, 'king'.

        Take care …

        The soldier leads HELEN *from the hut, and throws her at*
        MENELAUS' *feet. She slowly gets up.*

HELEN   Menelaus, you scared me half to death,
          sending in your man like that, without any warning,

        She moves to touch him but he recoils.

        So you hate me that much, do you?
        I suppose you'd like to see me dead …

MENELAUS   Your life and your death,
          for what they're worth,
        Are in my hands.
        It's a disgusting situation, isn't it?

HELEN   Let me speak up in my own defense.
        There are two sides to every story —
          maybe more.
        If you kill me it will be a terrible mistake.
        I will die in utter, devastating innocence …
        I, Helen, who am half divine!

        The CHORUS *shrieks in mock indignation at such a thought.*

CHORUS   There are two sides to every story ... [7]
          Maybe three ... [8]
          In this case, maybe more ... [9]

MENELAUS   I'm not listening.
           I came to do what must be done.

HECUBA   Oh for God's sake, hear her out, Menelaus!
           She mustn't die without having her *say*!

MENELAUS   All right, let her have her say.
           But nothing she says will carry any weight
               with me.

HELEN   *assuming her most dramatic stance*
           I know you hate me, Menelaus!
           Think whatever you will of me ... I understand.
           Maybe you'll never speak to me again.
           Maybe you won't even believe me,
               but listen, listen ...
           Here's what *really* happened ...

           pointing an accusing finger at HECUBA

           She's responsible, to begin with!
           To begin with, and first of all –
               she gave birth to Paris
               in the first place.
           Yes, despite the prophecies, despite the fact
           that he was fated to bring disaster!
               Think on *that*,
               and then consider ...
           Three goddesses offered Paris
           A choice of three wonderful gifts –
           Military conquests!
           Fabulous wealth! –

           One of the CHORUS *holds out a small bronze mirror and she studies herself.*

           – Or a gorgeous woman. In this case – me.
           He chose the last gift, naturally.

71

It wasn't *my* fault!
We women live beneath the shadows of men.
Like bugs we dwell in darkness;
   we have no shapes, we have no souls,
We fight among ourselves because we can't
   locate the enemy,
   Is that not so, sisters?

The CHORUS *giggles and murmurs in affirmation.*

HECUBA   You've memorized my own words well.
But from your mouth, Helen, they sound unreal.
Everything from your mouth sounds unreal.
I hear what I don't want to hear,
   I know what I don't want to know...

to herself

Have I been wrong, then —
Cassandra ... Andromache ... Helen?
Wrong about everything?

HELEN   Just think, Menelaus — if Paris had chosen
     otherwise,
Greece would now be ruled by Troy!

MENELAUS   *baffled by this convoluted logic*
What?

HELEN   What was I to do?
There I was — (a child of heaven, half-divine)
— abused, dishonored, and all because
   of my impossible beauty!

pausing for effect

I suppose you're wondering why
I ran away with him that night. Well I'll tell you!
He came for me — that *son of Hecuba* —
   and he had a powerful goddess with him.
I was helpless under her spell. And *you*, Menelaus —

you left him in the house with me
While you went off to *Crete* of all places!
Blameless, I tell you, I was blameless,
I was an instrument of Fate,
of History ...

CHORUS Time has learned nothing ... [1]
We have learned nothing ... [2]
History is a spider's web ... [3]

MENELAUS *screaming*
You stayed here *after* Paris was killed!
Why didn't you escape? You *stayed here*!

HELEN Escape? Escape? Oh God, how I *tried*!
I lowered myself out of my window by ropes
    more than once!
The guards discovered me and hauled me back in!
Imagine it, – there I was, dangling in mid-air,
Trying to get back to you, Menelaus!
   I felt like a spider
   suspended by its thread,
Suspended over those dreadful, dizzying walls!...

She breaks out into loud sobs. The CHORUS *mockingly copies
her, sob for sob.*

Menelaus ... I'm a child of heaven, half-divine!
But I'm a *woman,* a woman abducted by violent men!
And all because of this cursed beauty
   which should have been my glory!
I'm a victim of my own *divine loveliness.*
   Oh God!

HECUBA *raising her arms for silence*
Enough!
Shut up, you filthy little liar,
You disgusting 'half-divine' whore.
You and your 'divinity' – it makes me sick!
If this is how the gods move through man,
   who needs the gods?

CHORUS *shrieking in dismay*
Blasphemy, blasphemy! *all*

HELEN *throwing her arms around* MENELAUS' *neck*
Stop her, Menelaus! She's evil, she's ugly,
She's a *spider*!

HECUBA If the gods move in *you,* you bitch
Then I say be damned to them ...

HELEN She's crazy! Make her go away!

disengaging herself from MENELAUS

I am Helen. I don't tell lies.
I *alter* truth sometimes, until it suits me.
When I tell untruths, I tell them beautifully ...

CHORUS She tells them beautifully, beautifully ... [4]

HELEN I am Helen. I am a child of heaven!
I am half-divine!

addressing the CHORUS

I am Helen. I am above the Law.
I am beautiful because I *choose* to be!
Are any of *you* capable of judging me?

The CHORUS *remains silent, in mock defeat.*

Did anyone ever tell you, you silly children,
That the greatest triumphs might well be
   the merest, the simplest of lies?
But *I* don't tell lies.
I *alter* truth sometimes, until it suits me ...
My father, Zeus, is with me.
Many of the lesser gods are with me.
I am Helen. I am a child of heaven.
You can't approach me. You cannot judge me.

MENELAUS *turns, and faces the audience.* HECUBA, *moving*

74

in on HELEN, *finally stops and addresses her, face to face.*

HECUBA If you would only use
      what we call
      for want of a better word, my dear –
Your mind – then you'd realize
That nothing is more obscene, more naked
Than a lie.
A lie is a bilious green snail
Insinuating its way out of its shell.
It is superbly hideous, superbly fascinating.
Like a lot of things I know, it's so ugly
      it's *almost* beautiful …

She looks HELEN *up and down, making her meaning clear.*

Look at history, for instance. I'm starting to think
It's all a web of lies
Where all the gore becomes glory
In the telling and the re-telling
Of the lies.
Look at yourself, you fabulous bitch!
You'll probably be famous in years to come!
People like you never get punished for what they do.
It's as though you are meant to play
      some insane, historical role,
As though you can't do otherwise …
And everyone suffers as you sail through it all
Untouched, untarnished, ignorant.

chuckling

Gods are the fools that reside in our heads …

That means the gods *you* pray to, Helen,
Will not come through when you need them.
You project your petty, miserable mind upon them
      and they are maimed; they become
      as low, as despicable as you are.
They are reduced in power;
They may even cease to be
      as long as you abuse them …

staring into space, eyes wide

They may even cease to *be* ...

HELEN *laughs and begins to flirt with* MENELAUS, *stroking his head, etc.* MENELAUS *begins to weaken.*

to herself

And if I call upon *my* gods?...
The gods that live inside *my* head —
Will they still answer me?

pauses

The time has come
To blast all lies.
   Truth is, at the very least,
Endurable.
Or so I tell myself. *Helen!*

HELEN *and* MENELAUS *freeze.*

My son was a beautiful man.
He was all decked out in his shining armor
   when you first saw him.
You were lost, lady, lost within a glittering
   dream ...
What was Greece, then? — what was Troy?
   What was anything? Did anything
   really mean
   what it seemed to mean?

HELEN *still holding onto* MENELAUS
     I never loved him! I never loved him!

HECUBA Who cares what you 'loved'?
     You *wanted* to be free from Sparta,
     You *wanted* Paris, you *wanted* Troy,
     You *wanted* a series of recognitions
       of your miserable self!
     You suggest that my son took you by force,

by magic.
How come nobody in Sparta knew about it?
Didn't anybody hear anything?
Didn't you cry out that night?

HELEN, *trying to get away from her, climbs upon the rocks.*

You came here, Helen,
 dragging a war behind you.
War is a *word* for you, isn't it?
War is something that *men* do,
Something fabulous, something that history
 will glorify ...
I will tell you something I've only recently
 learned —
 war is blood and blood and blood,
 war is babies falling
 from the cradles of the sky.
War is the final nightmare.
The last sick page in a long sick story.
War is something that *we* do —
All of us, all of us ...

MENELAUS *turning around*
    But! —
    What did she do when she heard that *we*
     were winning?
    She stuck up for me, — (I heard about it) —
    She praised me in front of everybody ...

HECUBA When she heard that the Greeks were winning,
    you fool,
    She used your name in front of my son
    to torture him!
     But whenever *Troy* was victorious,
     she changed her tune.
    You see, Menelaus, she plays to win,
    And it doesn't matter what the game is.

CHORUS It doesn't matter what the game is ... [1]
    You play to win ... [2]
    You wait to see which way the tide

will turn ... [3]
That way you'll be sure to be on the
    winning side ... [4]
That way it won't matter how you
    change your tune ... [5]

HECUBA   *mockingly, to* HELEN
You lowered yourself over the wall,
You tried to escape,
Oh, help, help!
You were dangling in mid-air!
You were dangling like a spider by its thread!
Who ever saw you? Name one name!
When did it happen? Who were the guards?
Oh, why didn't you just go and hang yourself
While you had the chance?
I *begged* you to leave, remember?
I promised to help you sneak past the guards
So that we'd be left in peace.
But you'd have none of it. You loved it here
With the men of Troy
Kissing your feet. Didn't you, Helen?

HECUBA *rushes to grab* HELEN *bodily; members of the*
CHORUS *restrain her.*

And now you come out looking like this –
    all made up like a perfect slut,
And that disgusting dress slit halfway
    down your ass!

CHORUS   Let's have no *violence*! [6]
We are against violence! [7]
After all, this is *Troy*! [8]
We have no violence in *Troy* ... [9]

HELEN   *clutching* MENELAUS' *knees*
I am not a slut, I am not a silly bitch!
I am Helen, I am beautiful!

The CHORUS *releases* HECUBA *and returns to the rocks.*

HECUBA   She's had her say and I've had mine.
         Face the truth if you dare, Menelaus.
         Kill her. Don't be *violent*.
         Just kill her.
         The Law demands it.
         No one is above the Law.

         to herself and the audience

         But I no longer know what the Law is.
         I wonder if the purest evil might be
         The simplest of lies.
             Truth
         Is as short-lived as the sunrise ...
         I wonder if anything is good,
         If anything is 'evil'.
         I'm afraid. Maybe nothing *is*, maybe
         It's all madness. Maybe the gods are mad.
         Maybe there *are* no gods ...

HELEN   *to* MENELAUS
         Listen to her. She's going crazy.
         How can you believe anything she said?

MENELAUS   *without looking at her*
         You lied.
         You went with Paris willingly.
         You weren't enchanted. You lied.
         I lost my best men in this war.
         You lied!

CHORUS   War is sick. [1]
         War is a lie. [2]
         She had her reasons. [3]
         War needs no reasons. [4]

MENELAUS   Go away, just go away!
         I don't even have to kill you.
         There are many who are dying to see you dead.
         Go, just go!

HELEN *falling at his feet*
I kiss your feet.
I am Helen, I am beautiful. I am your wife ...
I don't have to die, I don't have to die ...

CHORUS *leaping one by one over* HELEN
Cities don't have to die ... [1]
Children don't have to die ... [2]
Gods don't have to die ... [3]
Myths don't have to die ... [4]
Truths don't have to die ... [5]

HELEN Shut up, shut up, shut up!

CHORUS *relentlessly*
Sing for Troy! [6]
War is sick; war is a lie. [7]
You have your reasons; *war* needs
no reasons ... [8]
History has its reasons, and
history doesn't lie ... [9]
It tells untruths,
It tells them beautifully. [5]

MENELAUS *She lied!*
I can kill her or enjoy her;
it's up to me.
My best men ...

pauses, gazing at HELEN

I think I'll *think* about it
And kill her later,
when we're far from Troy.
I'll take her to the beach,
I'll put her on my ship ... why not?
(she won't weigh down the ship), and then
I'll cope with things, I mean
I'll *cope* with truths and lies, —
Far away from here,
far, far from Troy ...

HECUBA   You loved her once.
          What's to stop you from loving her again?

MENELAUS I don't love her!
          I'm a military man, a man of strategy.
          I know *exactly* what I'm doing!

          MENELAUS *starts to exit in wrong direction, stage right,*
          realizes his mistake and exits stage left, towards the ships.

HELEN   *slowly getting up to follow* MENELAUS
          Beauty before age, Hecuba ...

          She exits and the soldier follows.

HECUBA   *after a pause*
          What were they all fighting for?
          It was not for Helen really, it was not for Troy —
              the altars, the towers, the dark mountains,
              the rivers of melted snow,
              the sacred temples of the dawn ...

CHORUS   Everything is gone,
          The laughter and the dancing in the night ... [1]
          The golden idols, gold itself, the gods ... [2]
          Power. [1] Sanity. [2] Glory. [3]
          Honor. [4] Gone! [5]

HECUBA   Everything I lived for — gone!
          I give over, I give in then — *I was wrong!*
          Who can I blame, then — who can I blame?
          The Greeks, the Trojans, the armies, Helen?
          All of us ... *all of us.*

CHORUS   Soon we will drift over the bitter sea
              in ships that look like giant
              angry birds ... [4]
          Towards the cloudy towers of Argos, or
              somewhere where alien riders
              ride along the shores ... [5]
          The naked children at our gates are

minus mothers! [6]
They are taking them down to the black ships! [7]
Where are they taking them? [8]
Stop them, stop them! [9]

TALTHYBIUS *enters, stage right, bearing the dead child. His
two soldiers follow, carrying a huge bronze shield, and the
child's small shield and sword. They prop these up against the
rocks and exit.* TALTHYBIUS *lays the child at* HECUBA's *feet.*

TALTHYBIUS   Hecuba, the last ships are waiting ...
The son of Achilles left very quickly,
     taking Andromache.
I was told that when she looked back to
     the shore,
     she screamed, and then she fell,
     got up, and fell again ... and then
     she spoke a kind of gibberish, and then ...

Well, what I mean is, they have sailed ...

speaking faster and faster and trying to avoid HECUBA's *stare*

She ... asked that Hector's shield be brought here.
She said: Use the shield to cover the boy
     when he's buried.
That's what she said: Use his father's shield.
She ... asked that he be given a decent burial.
He ... he fell from the tower.
He died instantly, *instantly,* I tell you!
It was not ... messy.

She said: Leave the boy in the hands of Hecuba.
     Tell her to wrap him up with
     whatever she's got.
That's what she said. That's what they told me.

We're going now to dig the grave.
As soon as he's buried we'll set sail.
Get him clothed and ready as fast as possible.
I've saved you some time ... I bathed him
     in the river on the way back,

I washed his wounds ...
Stop staring at me!

He exits in shame.

HECUBA *to* CHORUS
Put the shield down flat on the ground.

They do.

Bring clothing, bring flowers, bring anything
    You can find ...

The CHORUS *wanders around the stage, picking up*
CASSANDRA'S *flowers, rummaging around for bits of cloth,*
removing some of their own old jewellery, wordlessly
consulting one another as to their finds.

I don't believe this. I don't believe this!
This is not real. Nothing is *real*!

chuckling as she attempts to evade reality

That's it, isn't it? Nothing is real.
Therefore nothing matters.
Yes, I've got it now. Nothing matters.
And because nothing matters, nothing is *real* —
See, see?
This is somebody's dream. Yes, somebody's dreaming
And we're just dancing around inside his head.

She makes a few awkward dance movements.

See? I feel nothing. I'm just dancing.
Dancing around inside somebody else's head!

She looks at the child, screams, and throws herself to the
ground, thrashing about and moaning. Two of the women
restrain her before she injures herself in her wild grief.

I see soldiers, soldiers of *time*!
Armies of an improbable universe!

Forces of sickening, dizzying dark,
Enemies of everything that once was life!
  Mindless heroes who murder children,
  the seed of future worlds ...
Do you see, Cassandra? I too have visions!
I have visions of nothing, boundless,
  idiot *nothing*!
All truths, all laws, all beliefs are broken,
My mind is broken, my soul is broken.
My mind is nothing, my soul is nothing,
But *I* continue to be!
  How strange that *I* continue to be ...
Is there something, then, that can be
  called reality?

She quietens down, and the women release her.

Our lives are our lives.
And our deaths are our deaths. Possessing
  nothing else.
This is all we possess.
  The child possesses himself.
  Lead me back to the child.

*She bends over the body and begins wrapping bits of clothing
around it. The women pass the garments to and fro,
examining the quality, discarding some, muttering, shaking
their heads.*

What a useless death for you, you little thing ...
If you had fallen in battle,
  you'd have fallen as a king ...
But now you've no idea of the greatness of it all
If there is any greatness to it all,
  you funny little thing ...

There is no greatness to it all!
What is left from this glorious war? –
A broken child!

The stones of the walls have torn your
  hair out.

You used to have a bunch of crazy curls
That looked like a little garden
And I used to kiss you on your cheek
Where now a bone juts through ...

Cassandra was right
It is the same war, fought over and over
In all the bloody fields of history ...

Your arms are the same shape as your father's were
    and now they dangle from your shoulders,
    dead.
You proud little mouth is closed forever.
Did it clamp down on some final secret, child?
You lied, you lied when you crept into my bed
That strange turquoise morning, and you said:
    Grandmother, when you're dead
    I'll cut my hair
    And ride with the captains
    In front of your tomb.

She pats the child's face and hands and feet with a white cloth.

I clean your wounds. I make you whole.
The white cloth purifies the flesh which is
    the avenue to the soul ...

She runs her hand over the shield.

The print of his hand still shows on the handle
    and the dark golden stains of his sweat ...
Men and their disgusting toys of war!
Truth pursues them, history mocks them,
Fate dances like a dervish right before their eyes
And they revel in their savage joys
While worlds and dreams collapse around them
    and babies fall
    from the cradles of the sky ...
I give you these pitiful things —
Bits of cloth and dusty flowers.
But you possessed your life,
Now you possess your death —

85

therefore these things are yours.

The women bring a piece of purple and gold cloth.

This is what I thought you'd wear
When you grew up and married an exotic princess ...

She brings the cloth down over the body of the child.

With this child, I bury the future!

*Flashing lights indicate the fire which is the final destruction of
the city. The* CHORUS *looks back and gasps.*

So this place is lit, as you said, Cassandra,
With every conceivable color of Heaven and
    of Hell!
Are there no truths, then, are there no lies?
Wait – if there ever was a God
Then God's on fire,
God is the city!

CHORUS Time is flame, time is fire! [1]
        Troy is burning! [2]
        The fire eats the stones! [3]

HECUBA So all our prayers and rituals and sacrifices
        Were as empty and useless as skulls.
           The incense,
             and the bull's blood on the altars ...
        Nothing, all *nothing!*

*She takes a stone and throws it into the flame of the altar. The
fire is immediately extinguished.*

Fate takes us in its hands and hurls us to the ground.
    Our end
Is our splendor! History will remember us.
This is our destiny! Sing, women, sing!

There is dead silence.

Take the child to the grave.
He is finely clothed.
If the dead are finely clothed
  they have nothing to fear.
It's we the living
Who dread our pitiful dreams.

Members of the CHORUS *put the child's body on the shield
and carry him out. The rest of the* CHORUS *follows.*
TALTHYBIUS *enters bearing the mask of Poseidon under one
arm.*

TALTHYBIUS That's it, then. Look at it!
  Holy fire, unholy fire — who cares now?
  It's all over and we can go home.

HECUBA It's never over,
  And nobody ever goes home ...

TALTHYBIUS Come with me, Hecuba.
  Ulysses' men are waiting for you.

HECUBA So it's finally come —
  The hour of *reckoning*!

  laughing

  I guess it's better to know the truth
  Although, God knows — it's worse!

TALTHYBIUS Come *on,* Hecuba!

HECUBA Dawn will come.
  The fire and the darkness will be one.
  History is a spider's web,
    a circle of darkness
    a circle of fire ...
  All things are one!

  The flames rise higher with a mighty roar.

TALTHYBIUS Get *up,* Hecuba!

HECUBA *slowly rising*
If Troy is meaningless, then everything is
    meaningless,
    and that can't be.
I *demand* meaning. I *demand* it!

pausing

Smoke rises like dust and spreads its filthy wings.
I become a shadow, and the city disappears.
It falls on the threshold of Nowhere. It
    is a dream, an aftermath of flame.
Trees scatter black meaningless leaves
    to the wind,
Dreams scatter hopes, or lies.
Truth is as short-lived
As the sunrise ...

The stage darkens until there is only the dying fire and the hissing of the final flames.

TALTHYBIUS It's over, woman, it's over. Come ...

There is a great crash as the last of the wall gives way.

HECUBA Did you hear that?

TALTHYBIUS Yes. So? Other walls have fallen.
I am tired. You are tired. Come ...

HECUBA *chuckling dryly*
Lead on, my captor. On, to a new day.
On to slavery, on to the ships
    like giant angry birds
    that will carry us over
    the bitter sea,
Towards the cloudy towers of Somewhere,
Where alien riders ride along the shores ...

She exits.

TALTHYBIUS As the moon bends the oceans
            So this darkness bends the mind.
            Even the planets are weary.
            Everything awaits a series
                of wretched and unreal tomorrows.

            looking back for the last time on the rubble of the city

            Goodbye, you splendid towers,
            You once magnificent citadel,
            You horrible heap of stones ...

            Sing for the great city that cries out
                like a soul,
            That falls like a shadow
            On the threshold of Nowhere ...
            This place, this place was Troy.

            He places the mask of Poseidon on a rock, and exits. Light
            lingers for a moment on the mask. Then, darkness.

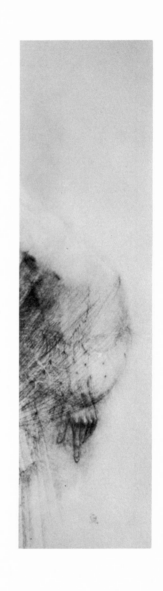

Orestes

A POEM BY YANNIS RITSOS

Translated by Gwendolyn MacEwen
and Nikos Tsingos

(Two young men, around twenty, stopped at the Propylaea with an air about them as though they were trying to remember or recognize something, even though everything was incredibly familiar and moving, though somewhat smaller — much smaller — than they had thought when they had been in exile, in another land, in another time — even the walls seemed much smaller, the enormous stones and the Lions' Gate, and the palace under the shadow of the mountain. Early summer. Night is falling. The private cars and big excursion buses have gone. In the quiet, the place breathes a deep ahh from the mouths of the ancient graves and memories. A piece of newspaper stirs on the burnt grass, blown by some vague breath. The night-watchman's steps are heard, and the big key closing the inner door of the castle. Then, as though released by the warm coolness of the night, the crickets beat their tiny drums. Somewhere, from behind the mountain, an uncertain brightness slinks — perhaps the moon. And at exactly the same moment, the sharp, rough wailing of a woman is heard from the stone stairway. The two men don't look at one another. They merge with the outer wall like two great shadows. After a time, one of them dabs the sweat from his brow with his scarf, points with a limp finger in the direction of the sound and speaks to his companion, who stands by, ever affectionately silent and devoted, like Pylades:)

Listen, she still hasn't stopped, hasn't tired. She's unbearable,
in this Greek night – so warm, serene,
so independent of us and indifferent, affording us
a little comfort – to be within it, to view it from the inside
and at the same time from afar; to see the night
stripped to the merest voices of its crickets,
to the sheer horrors of its black skin.

Oh, if only we too could be like that, independent, with the beautiful
joy of indifference, freedom from creeds, beyond everything,
within everything, within ourselves – alone, united, unbound,
without comparisons, antagonisms, rules, without being gauged –
by others with this or that expectation or demand. I just want
to see the strap of your sandal, which for me separates
your perfect big toe and points towards a place all my own,
towards a secret place, all mine, beside the rhododendrons,
add the silver leaves of night falling onto your shoulder
and the sound of the fountain passing imperceptibly under our toenails.

Listen to her, – her voice covers her like a profound resounding dome
and she is herself suspended in her own voice
like a bell-clapper, striking herself and ringing the bell,
though it's not for a holiday or a funeral, only the pure wilderness of rock
and below, the unassuming calm of the plain, underlining
this unjustified outburst, around which
the countless stars stir like innocent children's kites
with the everflowing paper rustling of their great tails.

Let's move on a bit so that the woman's voice won't reach us;
let's stop further down – not at the graves of the ancestors;
no libations tonight. I don't want
to cut my hair, – your hand has often
strayed through it. What a beautiful night –
something all our own, extending, branching out from us, sounding
like a dark river seeking the sea,
shimmering now and then beneath the branches in the twinkling of the stars
in this merciless, oppressive summer,
with occasional indetectable pauses, and chance leaps (perhaps someone

tossing stones into the river) – this little plashing
and down below the gleam of the wine-grower's window-panes. Strange,

a whole lifetime they prepared me and I prepared myself for this. And now,
in front of this gate I feel totally unready: –
the two marble lions – did you see them? – they've grown tame,
they, who started out so dauntless when we were children,
half wild, their manes bristling for some foolhardy leap,
now finally settled down agreeably on the two top corners of the outer gate
with dead hair, vacant eyes – terrifying nobody – wearing an expression
of punished dogs, – indeed, not even sad,
faithful, blind dogs, bearing no resentment,
their tongues licking from time to time the warm soles of night.

No, I'm not ready: – I can't; I don't have that essential
feeling of being at one with the surroundings, with time, with facts
and things, – it's not cowardice, – I'm unprepared
on the very threshold of action, a total stranger
in the face of the destiny others have assigned me. How is it that
others can bit by bit determine our fate, inflict it upon us,
and we concur? How can it be that with the merest strands
from some of our own moments they can weave
the whole of our time for us, coarse and dark, cast
like a veil upon us from head to foot, covering
every bit of our faces and hands, also, where they've placed
an unknown knife – totally unknown – its harsh glow
illuminating a landscape not our own –
this I know: not our own. And how is it that

our own fate complies with this, withdrawing,
and like an outsider gazing upon us and our alien destiny,
mute, austere, resigned, unparticipating,
without a sign of generosity or stoicism,
without even fading away, or dying,
leaving us prey to an alien destiny,
but *only one* – not hesitant and divided. Look at it lying there,
drowsy, – one of its eyes closed and the other dilated,
letting us watch it watching us and observing
our endless oscillating with neither approval nor disapproval.

I think that two counter-balancing forces are like our legs,
one force extending farther and farther away from the other
widening our stride to the point of dismemberment; and the head
is a knot still clinging to a sliced body,
while, I feel, legs are created to shift their position,
each one on its own, both in the same rhythm, in one direction,
to the plain below, beside the grape clusters, to the horizon beyond,
    now turning rose,
and thus transport our bodies entire; or maybe
we were created to take this terrible gigantic stride
over the unknown precipice, over the graves, even our own grave?
    I don't know.

But behind so many levels of confusion and fear,
    I can sense
the boundless silence spreading, – a justness,
an autonomous equilibrium which includes us
in the realm of seeds and stars. Did you notice? – at noon
as we were coming here, a cloud's shadow inched along the plain,
covering the wheatfields, the vineyards, the olive groves,
the horses, the birds, the leaves, – a diaphanous drawing
of a distant landscape of infinity, right here on the earth;
and the peasant proceeding along the edge of the plain
seemed as though he were holding under his left arm
the entire passing shadow of the cloud like a huge mantle,
magnificent, and yet as simple as his sheepskin.

Thus the earth familiarizes itself with the infinite, drawing something
from what is sky-blue and hazy; and infinity on the other hand
draws something from the earth, chestnut and warm, something from leaves,
something from earthen pitchers and roots, something from the eyes
of that patient cow (remember her?)
and from the sturdy legs of the farmer fading into the distance.

It seems like that woman will never stop. Listen to her.
Doesn't she hear her own voice? How can she remain
enclosed and suffocated in a single instant of a time long since past,
of feelings long since past? How, and with what can she

keep renewing this passion for revenge, this voice of passion
when all the echoes contradict her, even mock her; echoes
from the arcades, the columns, the stairs, the furniture,
the huge urns in the garden, from the caves of Zaras,
    from the reservoir,
from the stables of the horses lower down, from the guards' outposts
    on the hills,
from the folds of the female statues in the courtyard
and the noble phalli of the stone runners and discus-throwers?

You'd think that even the flower-pots in the house contradicted
    her wailings
with the indulgent nodding of a few sensitive roses
gracefully arranged by mother's hand
there, on the engraved chest of drawers in front of the great ancestral
    mirror,
in a double light, reflection upon reflection, watery —
    this I remember
from when I was a child — it's still clear to me —
watery glitter, delicate, neutral — a vagueness
something timeless, sinless — something gentle and wonderful
like the down on the necks of girls or the upper lips of boys,
like the odor of a freshly-washed body in the cool sheets
warmed by the breath of a summer's night, full
    of stars.

She understands none of this; not even the echoes
which mock her unlovely voice. I'm frightened; I can't
respond to her invitation — so overwhelming and yet
    so ridiculous —
to her worn-out, bombastic words which seem to be salvaged
from chests of 'the good old days' (as the old folks say),
like large, unironed banners into whose creases
mothballs, disillusionment and silence have penetrated — so old now
they don't even suspect their age, and they insist
on flapping with obsolete gestures above the unsuspecting
    passersby
rushing by exhausted, above the asphalt streets
which are modest, despite their width and size, with their elegant
    shop windows

full of ties, crystalware, swimsuits, hats, handbags, brushes,
better suited to the necessities of our time
and thus to the infinite necessity of the life which commands us.

And she goes on preparing mead and provisions for the dead
who no longer hunger or thirst and who have neither mouths
nor dreams of rehabilitation or revenge. She always appeals to
their infallibility (what infallibility, I wonder?) maybe to spare herself
the responsibility of choosing or deciding –
when the teeth of the dead, scattered in the earth
are stark white sowings in a boundless black valley
sprouting the only infallible, invisible white trees
that glitter in the moonlight, to the end of time.

Ah, how can her mouth stand those words,
salvaged, yes, salvaged from old trunks (like those
decorated ones with big nails), salvaged
from among mother's old out-dated hats,
which she no longer wears – she wouldn't stoop to that. Did you see her
in the garden this afternoon? – how lovely she still is – hasn't aged a bit,
maybe because she surveys time and realizes
every moment, – I mean that she renews herself,
aware of the youth she's losing – perhaps because of this she recovers it.

And mother's voice, it's so modern, everyday and precise, –
she can use, at will, the biggest words
or the smallest, with their greatest meaning, for instance:
'a butterfly's come in from the window,'
or: 'the world is excruciatingly marvellous,'
or: 'the linen towels should have had more bleach,'
or: 'a note from the fragrance of this night escapes me,' and
    she'll laugh,
maybe to prevent anyone else from laughing –

This profound understanding and tender leniency of hers
towards everyone and everything is almost contempt; I was always in awe
    and terrified of her

with her conscious lofty pride
as she mingled her cunning little many-sided laughter
with the tiny flick and flame of the match, lighting
the hanging lamp in the dining room, and there she was, lit up
    from below,
with the strongest light focused on her finely-drawn chin
and her delicate, palpitating nostrils, which for a while
would stop breathing and contract
as though she wanted to remain close by us, to stay, to be still
and not dissolve like a column of blue smoke into the breaths of night,
so the trees wouldn't carry her away with their long branches,
so as not to wear the thimble of a star for some endless handiwork —

That's how mother always found just the right movement and stance
exactly at the moment of her absence — I always feared
that maybe she'd vanish from our sight, or even vanish in an ascension — when
    she bent over
to tie the sandal which exposed her perfect,
painted, cyclamen-like toenail, or when she arranged
her hair in front of the big mirror
with such a charming, youthful and light movement of her hand
as though displacing three or four stars on the world's forehead,
as though placing two daisies together to kiss beside the fountain,
as though watching with affectionate boldness two dogs
making love right in the middle of the dusty street
in a burning summer noon. She was so simple and persuasive,
yet powerful, imperious, unexplored.

Perhaps my sister never forgave her for this — her eternal
    youth —
this woman both young and old, cautious because of opposition, denying
herself
beauty and joy — ascetic, repulsive in her
    prudence,
solitary and inconsistent. Even her clothes are
stubbornly old fashioned, sloppy, decadent, worn-out,
and the cord around her waist is loose, frayed,
like a bloodless vein around her belly (she tightens it, nevertheless)
like the cord of a sagging curtain which no longer closes or opens

revealing diagonally the landscape of an eternally harsh austerity
with steep rocks and huge trees, naked, entangled
against stereotyped, pompous clouds; and there in the distance
the undetectable presence of a lost sheep,
an animated white dot, a speck of tenderness — it can't be seen —
and my sister herself a vertical rock
encased in its hardness; — insufferable. Listen to her,
she's almost trivial: she criticizes mother and goes on provoking her
when she puts a flower in her hair or her bosom,
when she walks through the corridor with those deft, musical steps of hers,
when she bends over with a sorrowful ease, her head slightly slanted,
letting fall a sound with many meanings from her long earring
    onto her shoulder,
a sound which only she can hear — her sweet privilege. And my sister
    gets furious.

She keeps her wrath alive by the power of her own voice —
(if she lost that too, what would she have left?) — I think she fears
    the fulfilment
of punishment, to be left with nothing. Never did she
hear the nocturnal grass secretly rustling from the passing
of a supple, invisible animal in front of the windows,
    at supper-time;
she never saw the ladder, the one leaning without reason
against a high stark wall, on a leisurely day; she never noticed
that 'without reason'; she could never make out
the tuft of a corncob scratching the sole of a tiny little
    cloud,
or the outline of a pitcher against the starry sky, or an abandoned
sickle, beside the spring, one midday,
or the shadow of the loom in the closed chamber, when they're spraying
    the vineyards with sulphur
and the peasants' voices can be heard down below in the field,
as meanwhile a sparrow, all alone in the whole world,
nimbly picking away in the courtyard for insects, seeds, a few crumbs,
tries to spell out its freedom. She's never seen anything.

She's totally blind, imprisoned in her blindness. But how can it be
that she exists solely on her opposition to someone else,

solely on her hatred for someone else, and not on love
for her own life, having no attitude of her own? What do *they* want?
What do they want from me? 'Revenge. Revenge!' they cry.
Let them do it themselves then, since revenge sustains them.

I don't want to listen to her anymore. I can't stand it. Nobody
has the right to control my eyes, my mouth,
      my hands,
these feet of mine that walk the earth. Give me your hand. Let's go.

Long summer nights absolute, all our own,
intermingled with stars, sweating armpits, broken glasses, –
an insect humming softly into the ear of the quiet,
the warmed lizards at the feet of youthful statues,
the naked snails on the garden benches or inside the closed
      blacksmith's shop
promenading along the big anvil, leaving behind
white lines of sperm and saliva on the black iron.

If only we could leave the land of Mycenae again – how the earth reeks
      here
of copper rust and black blood. Attica's more cheerful. Isn't it?
      I feel
that now, this fateful hour, is the hour
of my final surrender. I don't want
to be their subject, their agent, their tool, nor
      their leader.

I've got my own life too, and I must live it. I don't want revenge; –
what can one more death subtract from death,
and a violent one moreover? – what can it add to life? Time has passed.
I no longer feel hatred – have I forgotten perhaps? Grown weary? I don't know.
I even feel some sympathy for the murderess; – she
      confronted great precipices,
great knowledge widened her eyes in the darkness
and she sees, – sees the inexhaustible, the unattainable, the unchangeable.
      She sees me.

I also want to regard my father's murder in the calm light
    of Death in general,
to forget it in the broad idea of that death
which awaits us too. This night has taught me
the innocence of all usurpers. And all of us are
usurpers of something, — some of peoples, some of thrones,
some of love and even of death; my sister
is a usurper of my one and only life; and I of yours.

Dear friend, how patiently you share with me
my foolish affairs. Nevertheless my hand
is yours; take it; usurp it (yes, you too); it's yours,
and because of that it's mine as well; take it; hold it tight;
you want it to be free from punishments, reprisals, memories,
free; — and that's how I want it also,
to be utterly mine, and only thus
to give it to you utterly. Forgive me
this secret solitude and sharing — you understand —
which tears me in two. What a beautiful night —

There's a damp scent of oregano, thyme, capers, —
possibly geraniums? — I confuse the aromas; sometimes,
blood smells like brine and sperm like a forest; —
a voluntary transference perhaps, — that's what I seek tonight,
like that soldier who spoke to us one night in Athens:
of how the seashore reverberated from the clanging and groaning,
and how he hid himself in the burnt bushes, above the beach,
gazing by moonlight at the wavering shadow of his sex
    upon his thigh
in an uncertain erection, struggling to *be,* testing
his will upon his own body, to transfer himself
from the field of death, into the hope of a dubious self-mastery.

Let's go further down: I can't stand to hear her; her wailing
assails my nerves and my dreams, the way those oars
beat against the floating corpses
lit up on and off by the torches of the ships,
    the shooting stars of August

and all of them glittering, young and erotic, incredibly immortal,
in a watery death which cools their backs, their ankles,
    their thighs.

How silently the seasons change. Night is suddenly falling.
A straw chair sits alone, forgotten beneath the trees,
in the fine dampness and the earth's vapors.
there's no distress; nor really any expectation; there's nothing.
A static movement extends into yesterday and tomorrow.
The turtle is a stone in the grass; after a while it moves –
a calm unexpectedness, a secret complicity, a happiness.

There's a kind of emptiness in your smile; – maybe because of
what I'm saying to you, and what I've got to say, and don't know yet,
haven't discovered yet in the rhythm of speech
that precedes my thought – very far ahead, – revealing to me
my own rhythm and my own self. Like once in the arena,
when the sweat-bathed runners arrived, and I noticed someone
who had tied a piece of cord around his ankle,
for no reason at all, on a whim. That's all there was to it. Nothing more.

Sacrifices, they say, and heroic deeds, – changing what? Year after year.
    Maybe we're put here for
these small discoveries of the great miracle
in which there is no longer pettiness or grandeur, killing or sin.

Everything is love – magic and wonder (as mother once said),
when the broad, fleshy, cool leaves of night
touch our foreheads, and the fruit that falls
is a message defined and incommunicable,
like the circle, the triangle, or the rhombus. I think now of
a saw which is getting rusty in an abandoned carpenter's shop,
and the numbers on the houses moving away to the horizon –
3, 7, 9, – the innumerable number. Listen; she's stopped.

An immense, impossible calm; – I think that thousands of jet-black horses

are darkly climbing up to Tritos, while on the other side
a river of gold is flowing down to the plain
with the dead springs, the uninhabited barracks and the stables
where the hay steams from an ancient heat from lost animals,
and the dogs, their tails between their legs, disappear
like dark smudges into the silver depths of the night.

At last, she's stopped; — quietness; — a redemption. It's beautiful.
Look at the shadows of the scurrying insects on the wall
leaving a small damp patch or a tiny little bell
which rings a little afterwards. Over there, a luminescence —
a prolonged, scarlet suspicion of a moon,
a minute, a solitary fire behind the trees, the chimneys of the houses,
    and the weathervanes,
igniting the big thorns and yesterday's newspapers,
leaving behind this acquiescence — which is almost glorious —
no expectations, no hopes, to proven futility,
right to the dauntless wilderness, to the edge of the road
with the spectral, violet passing of a cat.

When the moon rises, the houses sink into the plain below,
the corn creaks from the frost or from the law of growth,
the white-washed trees gleam at their bases like reaped columns
in a silent war, while the signboards of the small shops
hang like verified oracles over the closed doors.

The peasants will be sleeping, with their big hands
    on their bellies,
and the birds with their wee hands delicately hooked onto the branches
    in their sleep,
as though not trying to hold on, as though the effort
    were nothing,
as though nothing ever happened or is going to happen —
gently, gently, as though the sky has entered their wings,
and someone is going through the long narrow corridor holding a lamp
and all the windows are open, and you can hear the animals in the countryside
chewing their cud serenely, as if they're within eternity.

I like this fresh quietness. Somewhere close by, in a hallway
a young woman is probably combing her long hair,
and beside her washed, spread-out underwear is breathing in the moonlight.
Everything is fluid, slippery, cheerful. Big jugs, I think,
    in the bathrooms
must be spilling water over the napes and breasts of girls,
small, aromatic bars of soap slip onto the tiles,
bubbles ride over the sounds of the water and laughter,
one woman slips and falls,
the moon slips from the skylight,
everything slips on the soap — you can't hold onto anything
nor can you hold onto yourself; — this slipperiness
is life's returning rhythm; the women laugh,
shaking white, bubbly turrets of foam
onto the little forests of their pubises. Is this what happiness is?

This eve leaves me with an opening to the outside
and to the inside. I can't distinguish clearly. Maybe there are
huge deteriorated masks, metallic buckles;
and the sandals of the dead are warped from the dampness,
and move on their own, as though walking without feet — but they're not walking
and that large net in the bathroom — who wove it? —
knot by knot, — it can't unravel — it's black, — mother didn't
weave it.

A boundless shadow stretches over the arches;
a stone breaks loose and falls into the ravine — but nobody
    walks by —
then nothing; and again a branch breaks
from the frothy weight of the sky. Small frogs
leap lightly and soundlessly in the fresh grass. Quietness.

Grey mice fall and drown in the wells,
dense constellations flicker; they throw in
jugs, cups, mirrors and chairs from the banquets,
bones of animals, lyres and clever dialogues. The wells
    are never full.

Something like fingers of fire and coolness alternately passes over
    our breasts,
describing tracing circles around the nipples,
and we also flap around in circles, around a centre
unknown, indefinite, and yet defined; – endless circles
encircling a silent scream, a knife-wound; and it seems to me
that the knife is lodged in our hearts, making our hearts a centre
like the stake in the middle of the threshing-floor up there, on the hill

and around us are horses, ears of wheat, winnowers, muledrivers
and women-reapers beside the haystacks, with the moon's head
    on their shoulders,
hearing the neighing of the horses to the limits of their sleep,
the pissing of bulls in the wattles and the bushes,
the centipede's thousand legs upon the jug,
the slithering of the tame snake in the olive grove
and the creaking of the warmed stone as it cools down and contracts.

A word of love is always locked in our mouths, unutterable,
like a pebble or a nail in our sandal; you are reluctant
to stop and take it out, to undo the straps,
to lose time; – the secret rhythm of the course has overtaken you
and is greater than the annoyance of the pebble, greater than
the nagging reminder of your fatigue,
your procrastination; and still there is
some small, prickly delight and recollection
because you happen to have kept this pebble from a beloved beach,
from a pleasant stroll with lovely meditations, watery images,
when the chatter of the tobacco-merchants was heard
    from the seaside tavern
mingling with the song of the sailors and the song of the sea
far, far away, lost, near, alien, ours.

The poor thing has finally quietened down. In her silence I seem to hear
    her justification –
she's so vulnerable in her wrath, so wronged,
with her bitter hair falling onto her shoulder like
    funeral weeds,

walled up in her narrow justice. Perhaps she's fallen asleep,
and is dreaming of some innocent place with gentle animals,
and white-washed houses, with the fragrance of hot bread
    and roses.

And just now I've recalled — I don't know why — that cow
we saw one evening in a field in Attica — remember?
She was standing there, just unyoked from the plough, and was gazing far off,
steaming, with two small fumes from her nostrils rising
in the crimson, violet, golden sunset; she was dumb, wounded
in the ribs and the back, beaten on the forehead,
perhaps comprehending denial and submission,
irreconcilability and enmity meeting in agreement.

Between her horns she held
the heaviest part of the sky like a crown. After a moment
she lowered her head and drank water from the stream,
licking with her bloody tongue that other
cool tongue in her watery image, as if licking
extensively and calmly, maternally and inevitably,
her inner wound from the outside, as if licking
the huge, silent, circular wound of the world; — maybe
    to quench her thirst as well —
maybe only our own blood can slake us — who knows?

Afterwards she lifted her head from the water, touching nothing,
she herself inviolate and tranquil as a saint,
except that between her legs, as though rooted in the river,
a small lake took shape from the blood of her lips,
    a red lake
that worked itself into the outline of a map
that little by little spread out and dissolved; it vanished
as though her blood flowed far away, liberated, without pain,
into an invisible vein of the world; and that's exactly why
she was so serene; as though she'd learned
that our blood cannot be lost, that nothing can be lost,
nothing, nothing can be lost within this great

inconsolable, merciless and incomparable nothingness,
so sweet, so consoling, so nothing.

This nothing is our familiar endlessness. In vain then
this gasping, this anxiety, this glory. I drag along
one such cow with me, in my shadow — untied;
she follows me on her own; — she's my shadow on the street
when the moon's out; she's my shadow
over a closed door; and always, you know,
the shadow is soft, bodiless; and the shadows of her horns
might even be two pointed wings that could let you fly
and maybe you could enter the bolted door by another way.

And just now I've recalled (though it means nothing) the eyes
of the cow, — dark, blind, enormous, curved outwards,
like two small hills made of darkness or black glass; a belfry,
and the starlings who were sitting on its cross
were faintly mirrored upon them; and then someone cried out
and the birds left the eyes of the cow. I think the cow
was the symbol of some ancient religion. Such ideas and abstractions
are far from my thinking. An ordinary cow
is for peasants' milk and the plough, having all the wisdom
of hard labor, patience, usefulness. But yet,

at the last moment, just before the cattle returned to the village —
    remember? —
she let out a spasmodic mooing sound towards the horizon,
so that the branches, the swallows, the sparrows,
the horses and she-goats and peasants scattered all around,
leaving her alone in a stark empty circle,
from where a gang of constellations rose up
higher and higher into space, until finally *she* ascended; no, no,
I suppose that my eyes singled her out from the herd
mounting the shrubby path towards the village,
silent, docile, in the hour when the lamps were lit in the yards,
    behind the trees.

Look, day's breaking. See there, the first rooster's crowing on the hedge.
The gardener's woken up; he'll be propping up a small tree in the garden.
    Familiar sounds
from the work-tools — handsaws, pickaxes —
and the tap in the yard; someone's washing; the earth smells;
the water boils in the kettles; the gentle columns of smoke rise
over the rooftops;
there's a hot odor of sage. So we've gotten through
    this night also.

Now let's lift up this urn containing my hypothetical ashes;
soon the scene of my recognition will begin.
They will all find in me what they are waiting for,
they will find the just man, according to their terms,
and only you and I will know that in this urn
I keep, in truth, my real ashes — only the two of us.

And when the others triumphantly celebrate what I have done, the two of us
will weep upon the splendid, bloody sword, deserving of glory,
and cry for these ashes, this dead man, whose place
was taken by another who completely covered his flayed face
with a gold, honorable and reverent mask,
useful perhaps, with its clumsily-cut features
as an instruction, an example, an intoxication for people, a threat
    to tyrants,
an exercise that moves history forward, slowly, heavily,
    with each successive death and triumph,
not with any terrible knowledge (unachievable for the masses)
but with a difficult act, an easy faith,
inflexible and vital, an unfortunate faith,
a thousand times denied and another thousand times kept
by tooth and nail in the soul of man — an ignorant faith
which secretly accomplishes great things, ant-like, in the darkness.

And I the unbeliever choose this (the others don't choose me), though
fully aware. I choose
the knowledge and the act of death which elevates life. Let's go now —
not for my father, nor for my sister (Maybe the both of them

should cease to be one day), not
for revenge, nor for hatred — not for hatred at all —
nor for punishment (who should punish whom?)
but perhaps to complete a determined period of time, to
    set time free,
perhaps for some useless victory over the first and last
    of our fears,
perhaps for some 'yes', which glows hazy and indisputable
    beyond you and me,
to allow this place to breathe (if possible). Look how beautifully
    the day breaks.

The mornings are a little damp in Argolis. The urn is
almost frozen, with some dewdrops on it
as though the rosy-fingered dawn, as they say, sprinkled it with tears
while molding it between its knees. Let's go. The predetermined hour
has come at last. Why do you smile? Do you consent?
Is it because of what you knew but never spoke of?
This rightful end — is that it? — after the more rightful battle?

One last time, let me kiss your smile,
while I still have lips to kiss. Let's go now. I recognize my fate. Let's go.

*(They move towards the gate. The guards step aside as though they'd been
waiting for them. The old doorman opens the big door, keeping his head
modestly bowed as if in welcome. Soon a man's heavy groan is heard, and then
the startled agonized shriek of a woman. A great silence once more. Except for
the audible scattered rifle-shots of the hunters in the plain below, and the
countless twitters of invisible sparrows, finches, larks, tomtits, blackbirds. The
swallows circle persistently around the northern corner of the palace. Unper-
turbed, the guards take off their caps and wipe the inner leather rims with their
sleeves. Then, right in the middle of the Lions' Gate stands a huge cow, gazing
straight up into the morning sky with her enormous, pitch-black, motionless
eyes.)*

Bucharest, Athens, Samos, Mycenae,
June 1962-July 1966

About the Author

Gwendolyn MacEwen was born in Toronto in 1941 and left school at eighteen to concentrate on writing poetry and fiction. Her work has appeared in the major Canadian literary publications, and is well represented in contemporary Canadian anthologies. Her collection of poetry, *The Shadow Maker*, won the Governor-General's Award in 1970. Her radio plays, verse dramas and documentaries are heard on CBC Radio and her poetry readings take her all across Canada.

Ms MacEwen has travelled extensively in Israel, Egypt and Greece and has translated many works by Yannis Ritsos. *Mermaids and Ikons*, an account of her travels in Greece, was published by Anansi in 1978. She is currently living in Toronto and working on a new novel.